Author, Ronald Rayner, scrying with one of the original of the seven crystal skulls in the manner of Druid High Priests.

Distributors.

Amazon and Amazon Kindle

Add Design. Telephone (UK) 0845-6436395 Email: info@add-design.co.uk

ISBN Number. 9780957393981

Publisher

Blackthorn Publishing Ltd, Third Floor, 207 Regent St. London.
W1B3HH United Kingdom

Spiritual and Metaphysical Poetry

The Tree of Life The Hermit Mindfulness

Meditation and Prayer

By

Sylvia Gladys Rayner Lady of Annesley Grange 2021

Design and Covers. Creative Photography. Craig Allen Rayner

The publisher would like to express 'a thank you' to the following companies discovered on the Internet whose excellent download facilities and illustrations gave the ideas that made possible creative compilation of the Covers of this book: www.canstockphoto co.uk. https://pixabay.com and www.gettyimages.com Note. This book was produced during the Pandemic and Lockdown. Special thanks to Nielsen Book Data and Images Teams.

Printer. Colt Press Ltd, Unit 5 Ballingdon Hill Industrial Estate, Sudbury, Suffolk. CO10 2DX. United Kingdom.
Telephone. 01376-533300. www.colt-press.co.uk

FORWARD BY ALIEN MONK – SUN LIN

Welcome to a world of which you are probably unaware. A world from where you can draw comfort and confidence whilst others around you remain depressed. Be lifted up between Heaven and Earth; touching the supernatural. Avoiding dark places by developing a lasting sense of expanded awareness, and consciousness, becoming part of universal truth, and enjoying psychological transformation through mental focus; released from being a prisoner of everything in the past.

SOLVING THE MYSTERY OF CONSCIOUSNESS

Forward by world leading Mystic, Seer, Prophet, and Author Ronald Rayner.

Creative ideas provide the keys to connections of what, at first sight, appear to be unintelligible facts outside natural laws; raises them to the realm of 'difficult concepts', the solution to which can open the door to new discoveries – 'priori' ideas of subconscious intuition from the multiplicity of the psyche of the Paranormal. I can confirm personally, that God, the Powers of our Universe, communicates and instructs to me personally through the Paranormal.

My Predictions in the following pages will reveal to readers the reasons why they need to immerse themselves into a new way of thinking to ensure good mental health survives into Future Time.

We need a completely new way of thinking about communicating with Aliens, and being prepared for when this happens! Plus, are Aliens using Paranormal to interfere on planet Earth?

To: BECKY.
With great pleasure from
Ronald Rayner 10/6/22

Survivalist and Geographical Photographer Craig Allen Rayner on his way to Everest

INTRODUCTION

My sixty years of research and study of the paranormal phenomenon began when I was twenty years old and was working on shift at the BBC TV News Studios, Alexandra Palace, Wood Green, London (before the move to Television Centre) filling in the hours between rehearsals and transmission of news bulletins. Unwittingly, after writing ten books around the subject, I have become acknowledged across the world as one of the world's leading Visionaries and Seer reinforced by near one hundred percent accuracy in predicting events in future time. Over these years I have become convinced that there exists another dimension, the Fifth Dimension, completely outside and not constrained by Einstein's formula- energy equals mass times the speed of light squared, whereas the Fifth Dimension is Instantaneous to Infinity, in a different segment of reality that does not violate laws of Time and space.

This book introduces: The Rayner Theory of the Paranormal, Extra Sensory Perception, and Synchronicity – all part of the Fifth Dimension, the realisation of which will change our attitudes towards religions and belief systems.

We are, all of us surrounded by the paranormal because it is a shadow attached to every human being, through life, but only a tiny fraction of the world's population is aware of this magical Fifth Dimension, our life's shadow that accompanies us into death and beyond.

To shine a light on the Paranormal phenomenon is to illuminate ignorance of the actual truth of segments of reality surrounding us in our daily life, most of which is beyond most people's understanding. For example, most scientists do not see beyond Einstein-energy equals mass times the speed of light squared. A formula what places absolute limits on everything that we can do on the planet, and in space. The Paranormal on the other hand is free of mass and whose speed is instantaneous over any distance and any part of the world or space to Infinity. Paranormal = Instantaneous to Infinity. This formula changes everything we have ever understood because it is another segment of reality outside Einstein: a Fifth Dimension without limitations revealing the potential for contact with Alien and understanding Alien Abduction in the Paranormal. A phenomenon that is beyond most people's understanding of reality, where for example, some individuals can project thoughts or happenings into the minds of others, or read thoughts in the mind of another, outside the senses through which we normally receive information, but by way of Extra Sensory Perception, a field of the paranormal, a phenomenon that most people do not understand. This book will allow the clouds to roll by and shine a light upon a new expanded reality that many people will enjoy enormously. The Sixth Mass Extinction, and Pandemics, predicted in my books, have fetched forward the greatest changes in the history of humanity set in Future Time into 'Now'.

PARANORMAL EXPLAINED
MIND IS NOT CAPTURED IN THE BODY

The Paranormal is not part of material consciousness and remains independent of the science of the material. Furthermore, paranormal events can take place whether the body is awake or in an unconscious state, even in coma. Here follows examples of awareness in an unconscious person separate from the normal, which I describe as a paranormal psychic phenomenon. Many years ago, I met with and talked to patients in two hospitals who had suffered a near death experience during surgery. Patients recalled that during their time in the operating theatre undergoing heart surgery, found themselves looking down from above watching in detail the surgeons and nurses carry out procedures, finding themselves back in their body after leaving the operating theatre. Clear proof of a split in their subconsciousness; one half remaining in the physical material world, the other half in the paranormal world outside space time, a synchronistic in another dimension. A form of consciousness outside a normal unconscious state. Neurologists will be quick to grab the explanation, 'There was clearly a lack of oxygen that confused the neurons in the brain' 'Not so, because how does a confused brain clearly see the personnel in the operating theatre carrying out medical procedures and record in memory, if the brain is in a confused neurological state.

Another example of the paranormal at work is vivid detailed memory of an alien abduction in the face of clear proof that the person claiming to have been abducted by aliens had not left their bed. Proof that Mind is not captured in physical.

The paranormal comes into function during part of the sleep cycle. People in general dream throughout most of their sleeping hours, but do not remember their dreams except for REM sleep. This period of sleep occurs during rapid eye movement when the physical body is in a state of paralysis. Dreams during REM sleep can be vivid and bizarre. In rare cases people with a powerful mindset can pick up memories left behind in the minds of others of someone who has died, more particularly Mediums working to contact a deceased, through the Paranormal, after that person's death.

It is interesting that women in general are more disposed to take an interest in expanding conscious awareness, consequently women tend to make the best Mediums, Clairvoyants, and Visionaries.

Paranormal teaches everyone to enjoy every minute of every day by seeing the beauty in all things, and becoming aware that their personal potential is greater than they think. I have laid out in detail, together with my explanation of fourteen categories of the paranormal phenomena and Extra Sensory Perception and Synchronicities, plus simple tests that can be used by readers and their friends to discover who has an inherent talent for clairvoyance and more. Please take my test seriously, and keep accurate records, with the reward that you will raise much fun and genuine enjoyment as friends realise that there is so much more to their inner self than that of which they were aware and realising there really is much to be gained personally by expanded consciousness and self-awareness. I do not recommend discussing this subject with husbands many of whom will be dismissive of a subject about which they know absolutely nothing, but the idea that their wife could develop a greater conscious awareness than themselves would be unthinkable; dismissing of the fact that female clairvoyants have used their gift to help police solve a murder. What more proof do we need.

For this book I made my usual out of the body experience in the Paranormal to visit Alien Monk Sun Lin in his studio, in Lhasa, Tibet. It was a sad experience, and I fear for the future of Tibet. China appears not to realise that they have control of one of the major tourist attractions in the world, but life for Tibetans is becoming more restricted. China must be recognised for the good that they have brought to Tibet. No longer the unacceptable death rates of mothers and babies due to lack of midwives and medical care, formally one of the highest mortality rates in the world. Today they have clinics, medical care, and hospital care. I also must doubt the idea of thousands of able-bodied young men sitting, chanting, in Monasteries, instead of planting and working in the fields to produce food for a population in poverty, and often near starvation. Monks trooping round with their bowls to receive rice from villagers who had virtually nothing for themselves.

I am also unhappy with the way they have developed their own unique side to the Paranormal. This is not in the Paranormal, but the product of very young minds.

The end is in sight and this cannot be attributed to China. Young men are increasingly seeking wine, women and song, in preference to sitting chanting in a Monastery.

In covering the subject of alien UFOs, and alien abduction in the paranormal, I am delighted to publish the story in her own words by: Tracey Fletcher, an experienced Clairvoyant who has worked with police in solving a murder, and qualifies to be taken seriously when recounting her own personal experience of a Paranormal Alien Abduction shortly after seeing an alien UFO whilst walking in her local park. Alien Abductions are fascinating, because they have the potential to reflection Alien intrusion into life in present time, and reflections of possible events out there in future time. Also raising the question; can Aliens manipulate life on Earth.

I was not surprised when, on my return journey, I encountered the 'Skull of Doom', who has made the most accurate predictions from Future Time since 2010. Predictions about the future, so accurate, they would be unbelievable if they were not recorded in print. He has made a personal campaign to protect me from harm by the evil all around. His predictions for the future are grim, and his marker of proof of Global warming appears to be the melting of the permafrost across Siberia that will place all those communities at risk.

I describe details of my own experience of speaking with God, plus an insight into the world of the unredeemed dead.

THE RAYNER THEORY OF EARTH MOON AND GAIA

People who are in contact with and use their Paranormal powers are a minority, who form a unique privileged society who enjoy feelings of elation from expanded consciousness, a phenomenon that outsiders will never understand, but this could be you.

Planet earth was evolving literally billions of years before the remains of early humans were uncovered by archaeologists around three million years ago. Planet earth is infinitely much older and wiser than humans who have only recently become aware that the Earth is an intelligent organism in its own right. Named Gaia, by the brilliant genius James Lovelock, the first scientist to explain how and why the earth is alive and transcends everything, constantly creating biosphere of particles acted upon by forces with a feedback that stabilises earth's surface temperatures, enabling life in all its forms on land and in the oceans; continuous production of food for everything and everyone. Clearly a cybernetic that has its own timescale and awareness, exceeding beyond that of humankind and billions of times more complex and entirely capable of anything everywhere able to trigger miniature Ice Ages for period of rest when a planet can heal and cleanse itself, and start all over again.

Gaia is a complex cybernetic linked with other cybernetics across the solar system, all communicating necessarily instantaneously because of the distances involved, rendering possible Communication with others in the solar system. Not by primitive radio and television transmission a primitive invention in communication by early man, but by finding a cybernetic to paranormal and using paranormal, but only those individuals with abilities in expanded consciousness, and Extra Sensory Perception, will be able to detect and understand the phenomenon.

What is important to cementing the Rayner Theory and moving beyond Lovelock is the fact that planet earth reproduces. Earth reproduces by giving off electrons singularly or in waves to its smallest nearest moon, [part of the theory is everything]. The giving of electrons to its Moon is proven by the Moon constantly moving further away from the Earth. Our Moon is Earth's twin, the same age, and composed of the same materials however, whilst the Earth has a very strong magnetic field that protects it from the radiation from the Sun, the Moon. being only around a fifteenth of the volume of the Earth, does not. The Moons tiny magnetic field fed by electrons from planet Earth is causing the Moon to shrink in size.

The moon is vital to life on Earth because its gravity hold keeps earth in an upright position, plus or minus seventeen degrees, which fetches regular summers and winters, vital to the production of food. As the moon moves away from earth, shrinks and loses its grip, planet Earth will flop over to its new horizon and Earth will follow the fate of Mars, the Moon will be influenced increasingly by the gravity of the sun and that will be the end of our solar system, as the sun expands and eats up all the planets in the solar system.

If you want to see into the unknown coming at us every day from future time, simply follow the instructions in this book by getting on to the starting line- practice Meditation into Mysticism.

THE RAYNER THEORY –
SCIENCE OF THE FIFTH DIMENSION

In the material physical world - everything is restricted by Einstein's theory: mass equals energy times the speed of light squared (relativity). In simple terms, travel in time is calculated and contained within its boundaries that the mathematical formulas will allow.

In the non-physical world-massless, the subconscious mind is unrestricted: instantaneous across time and space to infinity, enclosing past, present and future time, comprising the Rayner theory of the Paranormal, Extra sensory Perception, and Synchronicity, in its own segment of reality, that does not conflict with the fundamentals of space time.

In very truth, the Rayner Theory is new and an amazing breakthrough in science. It will change conceptions about the way the Universe in which we live works. My theory is actual, therefore fathomable, and possible. It is filling a gap in our knowledge that the transmission of information does not have to be identified with energy and mass, but is contained in a massless plain in which information is transmitted instantaneously, proving that ESP and Synchronicity are outside the known fundamentals of science, but all part of a different section of reality itself, a phenomenon that appears to be impossible is, in reality a nonquantitative different section of reality, the Paranormal, a Fifth Dimension.

There are myriads of concepts of reality, many of which are not owned by science alone, but that does not render research outside normal parameters of a laboratory inferior to science. Rather that it reveals the limitations of known science. For example, in specific experiments, scientists cannot tell us where an electron is, other than it can be anywhere or may even be a wave, and yet many scientists cannot accept that Paranormal, ESP, and Synchronicities are a similar situation. I have to confess that I have spent time trying unsuccessfully to come up with an equation moving on from mass equals frequency to massless equals instantaneous. **When science does eventually discover new particles, probably this year, such events will prove that there are different segments of reality.**

SCIENCE OF THE PARANORMAL HOW TO EXPAND
YOUR PERSONAL CONSCIOUS AWARENESS

Meditation (mindfulness and mysticism) can more efficiently link together the conscious mind with the subconscious mind, to evolve an expanded personal conscious awareness with expanded personal reality; all of which cojoin to produce a more confident and purposeful you, expelling depression and fear, and enabling connection to the Paranormal. The Paranormal consists of: Extra Sensory Perception, and Synchronicities, all outside mechanical physical reality. The Paranormal is not restricted by Einstein's theory of relativity- energy equals mass times speed of light squared, (short lived virtual particles that return the energy they borrowed and disappear) Einstein is governed by rules.

The Formula

PARANORMAL – EXTRA SENSORY PERCEPTION – SYNCHRONICITIES
MASSLESS = INSTANTANEOUS TO INFINITY

Non quantitative not violating the laws of Time and Space.

THE PARANORMAL has separate segment of reality because it is not mechanical or physical reality, it is massless, and instantaneous over and distance to infinity, is outside the normal parameters as understood by scientists and mathematicians in the present day, because it is outside the rules of space-time, but does not conflict with spacetime. Everyone has the potential to develop awareness of ESP by connecting their subconscious mind more fully to their conscious mind through Meditation and Mysticism to gain ESP, a true heightened awareness in the field of consciousness. There is nothing evil or anti-religious about ESP. On the contrary, those of us who do develop an awareness across ESP use this ability to help brothers and sisters in the world. ESP is a God given phenomenon to aid the very survival of mankind from earliest humankind. The paranormal is absolute proof of instantaneous communication across any distance, to God, through prayer, for example.

CONNECTING SUBCONSCIOUS TO CONSCIOUS

My findings over sixty-five years of research are that most people in the world are not aware of the hypothesis - Paranormal, Extra Sensory Perception and Synchronicity phenomenon, because their subconscious mind is not fully in touch with their conscious mind and not receiving premonitions, promptings, clairvoyance, all the phenomena that helped early man to survive and recover from very small tribal populations.

The good news is that many people can escape the machinery of physical existence by developing ESP from the simple practice of Meditation, a mental exercise that develops and fully connects the conscious mind to the subconscious mind, and opens the gateway to the Paranormal. Both men and women can enjoy the benefits from being attached to the paranormal phenomena, developing ESP through Mindfulness and Mysticism.

Everything can be achieved by individuals working in solitude in the quiet of their home, or living area. Some of the fourteen categories explained in this book lend themselves to sharing. I have described lists that can be used by a few people meeting together to reveal through simple tests those who have the potential to develop their talents further and practice Mediumship, Clairvoyance and much more.

THE RAYNER THEORY OF EXTRA SENSORY PERCEPTION
HIGHTENED AWARENESS IN THE FIELD OF CONSCIOUSNESS

Consider ESP a connection outside our normal senses, but in nature - our psychic to a greater completeness of experience and reality. When a person falls into a coma or is anesthetised during an operation, in some, consciousness is suspended and splits off as an Extra Sensory Perception, a phenomenon that is not part of an organic body as in nature such as automatic reflex, proof that we are not captured inside the body, for example: ESP is not in time and space, as in Einstein, but is a CAUSUAL SYNCHRONICITY lying in a Fifth Dimension, in its own segment of reality. A space continuum - no mass-formless-nonquantitative-instantaneous ordered - outside Einstein. A whole panorama of NEW, that can explain the unexplained, and can open a whole new panorama on life itself.

CONFIRMATION OF THE RAYNER THEORY

The beginning of knowledge is to Meditate, whatever religion, and no matter what is ones chosen faith, Meditate on the very concept of God, and find the meaning of cosmic consciousness by one's own personal experience; became immediately aware of the separation of the material physical world, and the world of spiritual matter, such as Paranormal, Extra Sensory Perception, Synchronicities; in a Fifth Dimension of reality Instantaneous, a new state of cosmic consciousness, direct insight where we can become aware of our Paranormal shadow that accompanies us through life; that breaks from the physical body on brain death, when we enter a world of time and space without physical, it confirms without question the Rayner Theory is real. The world of the physical, and the world of the ethereal. One dimension captured in Time, and Space, the other dimension Instantaneous to Infinity of present and future time, outside the physical, in its own reality. A Fifth Dimension revealing that there is no need to fear death.

JOINT ENTERPRISE
Does GAIA encompass EINSTEINS Relativity
or RAYNERS FIFTH DIMENSION

Any important addendum to the hypothesis of Gaia, is that Gaia regulates itself and reproduces. Gaia passes on energy received from the sun to its nearest smaller mass, passing on electrons in particle or waves to the Moon. This constant transfer of energy propels the moon away from Earth by a small amount every year, which is proof of continuous transfer and reproduction.

Gaia is more, not quantifiable. Its influence in time and space are instantaneous, without limit, without boundaries, continues by self-regulation, unlike Einstein-the physical governed by rules. To build upon and compliment that brilliant man James Lovelocks hypothesis of 'Gaia' it is necessary to look beyond Einstein to an intelligent self-aware super organism - RAYNERS FIFTH DIMENSION: Instantaneous, esoteric metaphysical metamorphosis, without mass or boundaries - The Paranormal, Extra Sensory Perception, Synchronicities, into Divine; everything contributing to existence. EINSTEINS DIMENSION IS - Mathematical in physically constraining time across space restrained within the calculations from the formula - Energy equals mass times the speed of light squared. All governed by rules. Not the Paranormal.

THE PROOF OF CONSCIOUSNESS SPLITTING OFF PARANORMALLY

In the sixties I carried through private research talking to good natured young surgeons at a hospital in North London and a hospital in Central London, all good-natured fellows to a man, but everything was off the record for the obvious reasons of guarding their reputations within strict NHS. To a man (no women) they described the rare patient who told them of their experience whilst anesthetised during an operation, becoming aware of themselves on the ceiling of the operating theatre looking down at the surgeon and nurses carrying out procedure on their body. One talked about listening to the anaesthetist calling for 'faster', "the patient's blood pressure is rising to a dangerous level" and other medical speak. Waking after the operation, patients were back in the room with clear detailed memory of watching the operation from the ceiling of the operating theatre, absolute and clear proof of consciousness suspended and splitting off as an extra sensory perception.

I have similar records from patients anesthetised for dental operations. Proof that we are not captured inside our physical body.

PROOF OF COMMUNICATION DIRECTLY TO THE POWERS OF THE UNIVERSE - GOD

Perhaps the greatest breakthrough in human history is my positive proof that the Paranormal communicates instantaneously, through time and space, providing absolute proof that Prayer or Repentance by any individual, or group, is in very truth transmitted instantaneously direct to the Powers of the Universe – God. Certifying that the claims by Prophets and leaders of religious communities made over the years from anywhere in the world have always been true. Proof that any person male, female, or child of any race colour or creed, however humble or lowly, whether in a place of worship, bedroom, train, bus or car can pray directly to God at any time of night or day.

What is amazing is that the Paranormal also reveals and confirms that no individual, whatever they may claim for themselves, can forgive the sins of another, without the 'sinner' first going through personal repentance, to ask for forgiveness of their sin, because every person has their own single personal Paranormal Shadow that cannot be interfered with by another. This is an immutable fact.

It is not my place or wish to tell full or part time professionals, in any sphere of religion, how to act, or how to do their job. I will confess that I, personally, served for a few years in their position, including taking Communion and Confession.

What I learnt over those years is; before making a request in Prayer for help from God, one must do everything in one's own power a solve the problem, only then ask the Holy Spirit for help. Say the Prayer, and a Synchronicity will usually arrive to fetch a solution. Another certainty is that Science is God's gift to religion, and that ancient new or old Testaments, and other religious texts, must not be used to overrule scientific proof - facts; of that I am certain.

WOMEN HAVE THE ADVANTAGE WHEN IT COMES TO ESP.

TAKE THE SIMPLE TEST AND DISCOVER THE HIDDEN YOU.

Women are superior to men in the field of the Paranormal, and Extra Sensory Perception, and Synchronicities, because women are more open minded, sympathetic, more outgoing, and great listeners when it comes to learning something to their advantage. This is why I urge women to come together, and use the Test I have devised to discover hidden talents that can be developed to advantage. If a talent is only marginal, that talent can be improved fifteen percent by practicing the skill that has been uncovered.

PARANORMAL* EXTRA SENSORY PERCEPTION *SYNCHRONICITY CATAGORIES

Apparitions- ghosts (see psychokinesis)

Clairvoyance- mind to mind communications

Meditation- cognition- psychotherapy

Mediums- sensory echoes of the dead

Mindfulness- an extension of meditation

Mysticism- intuitively seeing expanded reality

Out of the body- split consciousness

Precognition- ESP heightened awareness

Psychokinesis- mind projected phenomena

Reincarnation-moving on after the paranormal leaves our physical body

Scrying- mind merging instantaneously with external fields

Synchronicity- consciousness merging externally

Telepathy- information Paranormally

Universal Collective Subconscious- unified field of consciousness

MEDITATION

USING THE POWER OF OUR MIND TO GUIDE OUR LIFE

WHY MEDITATE?

The whole history of the UK going back centuries, particularly during the rigidity of disciplined Victorian and Edwardian eras, both at home and in schools, closed off and prevented the minds of the public, and children, from developing expanded awareness and consciousness [children should be seen and not heard, don't speak unless spoken to]; [no votes for women] has led fundamentally to wide spread mental ill health problems in modern times. The closed and narrow thinking by our 'elders and betters' has prevented people from experiencing freedom of mind that develops into happiness, and a feeling of freedom in daily life.

All contributing to weakening peoples' ability to cope with problems such as 'Lockdown'; not seeing loved ones and friends. When I was four years old, I was walking to school during Air Raids throughout the Second world war. I hid behind front garden walls when German bombs were falling all around. I also survived the years of shortages of food during the war.

People today have been 'molly coddled' over the years and are not as strong as were we. Nevertheless, we still have to love and care for everyone, whatever race colour or creed. We are not allowed to give them a kick in the backside and say, "this is what it is, just get on with it", as my teacher said when I started crying in class after seeing my best friend, and his mother, killed by a bomb on their way to school.

USING THE POWER OF THE MIND TO INFLUENCE LIVES

INTRODUCTION

Anyone who desires to get rid of the burden of anxiety and fears of everyday life successfully, by taking on spirituality in order to connect with the Divine must not treat meditation as a tourist, selfishly taking a quick look, and moving on.

Readers serious about changing their life for the better should treat Meditation as a pilgrimage, and mould it into their everyday for the longer term.

WHILST I HAVE LISTED THE CATAGORIES WITHIN THE PARANORMAL IN ALPHABETICAL ORDER, I HAVE LIFTED OUT AND PLACED MEDITATION TO THE FORE BECAUSE IT IS THE NATURAL STARTING PLACE FOR NEWCOMERS TO THE PHENOMEMON.

MEDITATIONS - LONG TERM BENEFITS FROM DEVELOPING A BALANCED MIND AND OUTLOOK ON LIFE

One of the long-term objectives from the practice of Meditation is the development of a balanced mind and personality because even a mild personality disorder can cause disadvantages in long term employment, family life, marriage, and many aspects of everyday life, people completely unaware that it is their own personality that is causing problems, often leading to mental illness; initially brought about by really poor parenting, sometimes fetching difficulties through schooling with problem teachers or bad personal behaviour fetching confrontation with police.

FACING UP TO TRUTHS ABOUT PERSONALITY COGNITION SOLVING THE MYSTERY OF CONSCIOUSNESS

Perception and reasoning- the process by which knowledge in acquired forms in the mind a mental map of immediate surroundings, and environment. A picture painted in the mind must be related to the truth because, if an individual's interpretation of the reality is distorted or incorrectly interpreted compared to the facts, and reality, that individual is in danger of developing a personality disorder that plays out in everyday life, fetching all manner of problems that would normally be avoided.

PHYCHOTHERAPY

It is important to see the world around you as it really is in correlation to the facts and very truth. Basically, the truth about oneself; personal behaviour and attitudes towards others.

The realisation and understanding one's faults and shortcomings can bring what feels like miraculous changes. Our path through life need not be a route past daily conflict, needless disagreements, and arguments with others; avoiding dreaming up needless insurmountable difficulties that exist only in the mind. Hatred of someone for no apparent reason, resulting in nervousness and lack of confidence. All of these problems can be helped by Meditation, facing up to the need for a renewed purpose in life. To do harm to no one, and be the best one can be every day.

I am going to repeat myself in order to get the benefits of Meditation home to readers. (1) Meditation is a practice that calms mental activity and reduces visual stimulation by closing the eyes. (2) Relaxes and eases tension in muscles throughout the body. (3) Evaporates feeling of aggression and fear. (4) Can give rise to feelings of wholeness never before experienced. (5) Chanting Om or God out loud or under the breath opens up neural networks in the brain, sooths and calms by producing Alpha waves, proof of beneficial phycological effects on the brain.

(6) Practitioners will emerge over time with a renewed personality. Calm, more confident, more optimistic and unafraid of what tomorrow might bring because of problems in the past that could not be solved; the problems now seen in the light related to very truth.

HIDDEN POWERS OF MIND
HAPPINESS COMES FROM THE MIND

Mind has greater powers and reach than is generally realised. Able to interact with external fields after a short period of Meditation that costs nothing more than personal effort and time. The mind can be trained to project into mysterious fields such as mysticism, and the Paranormal, subjects covered in this book.

If you cannot progress with our OM MANI PADME HUM try humming this tune, "I sing the song my saviour sang to me, how sweet thou art, how sweet thou art", over and over again. It will solve your problem.

Extract - ALIEN MONK 2 2010
MEDITATION

I'm going to stick my neck out in my own inimitable way in my search for the truth and state that most books written about meditation presume to offer too much, whereas, in reality, adherents often gain very little. It is not that the promises are not true, one of the problems is that writers use eastern names and words that sound silly, and used for no other reason than grabbing authority for themselves or their book. In truth, their clever words and names are nothing more than a distraction. Their promises of successful results, overnight, are probably the biggest cause for disappointment.

I am going to avoid their paths by sticking to the facts, and moving ahead at a steady pace at which everything can be easily understood. My advice, however, is to settle down to the idea that 'getting into this', is going to take a few weeks of effort. Albeit that no one has to sit cross legged on the floor or join a group. The attraction of meditation is that it can be practiced by anyone, at any time, in any place, including the home.

I good start in a preparation for meditation is to sit relaxed in a comfortable chair, and simply contemplate. Sometimes this is not possible for busy people with families, and they may have to snatch time on a train journey to meditate, and why not. What is important is to make a start and exercise patience because nothing is going to develop overnight. If a noise that cannot be overcome is a problem, commence by chanting, OM MANI PADME HUM quietly to yourself until your mind stills.

Gently push away to one side thoughts about worries, anger, or anxiety. If you fall asleep, that is great too, because at least you will have enjoyed some benefits from your start up. When the mind becomes stilled, do not allow your thoughts to wonder. We are now at the beginning of mind control. If nothing works, because your mind continues to race out of control, you should avoid meditation and replace meditating with the thought that you, by your own volition, have decided to conquer and control your mind. Having reached this point, you have not failed. Just hang in there and experience emptiness or nothingness. Having reached this far and have not given up, you have passed the test, because you really are making an effort to embark on an experience that is unfamiliar to you. Congratulate yourself.

Succeed in these efforts, and the prospect of control is in sight, and you may even become a different person, perhaps the wonderful person lurking inside you that has always been trying to emerge, but held back through anxiety and lack of confidence, possibly due to someone or the people around you continuingly criticising you or telling you that you are no good, just to put you down. Remember, one of the benefits is that you are on the way to seeing yourself and others from the point of being an observer, and this will enable you to reach towards your true potential; the really great you.

Focus on controlling your thinking and you will also see the wisdom of avoiding situations or people that make you unhappy. You will replace them with a feeling of calm and confidence. Avoid evil argumentative troublemakers like the plague. And there are plenty around. Try to seek out causes of your worry by looking into the darkest corners of your mind, everything will then appear in its true perspective and much of the dread will fall away. Meditating whilst walking, reciting the mantra, Om Mani Padme Hum, is another way of achieving a happy tranquil state of mind, by pushing aside troublesome thoughts and worries.

Keep meditating and the wonderful qualities of the true you will reveal themselves. You will develop the ability to understand and read the thoughts and motivations of others, and identify the evil ones. You will also learn to understand your own true motives, almost like an observer of yourself, which will lead to an improved you. Perhaps the most important lesson to learn is that in spite of the opinions of others, however close to you, your true self is always there. A new and different you, will begin to emerge, and appear to others as a loving, caring voice and heart; albeit that some people are so confused in their own personality, they will begrudge you any praise, even when its due. Try to avoid them.

When men were able to extract metal ores from the ground, a new age began. When meditation lights up the darkest corners of your mind, a new life for you will begin. When you are able to draw out the sword captured in the stone, you will reveal to yourself that you have become part of the all-embracing light – you are as good as anyone around, perhaps better.

APPARITIONS

Apparitions are reported across history in every culture around the world, usually of a very short duration and without any meaning or useful purpose or explanation and leaving no trace.

Most people see a deceased person and believe it reveals the survival of the dead. This is not true because apparitions are a visual hallucination, albeit that they are very varied and have been known to include animals. Usually occur upon waking. Reach out to touch or speak to the Apparition, and the image will disappear immediately.

APPARITIONS AND GHOSTS

The human mind is so complex and powerful in the dream state, whether it occurs during natural sleep, under sedation, after a stroke; becomes the world that exists for the dreamer. Albeit that the world in which the dreamer is living clearly is totally imaginary, and does not exist in reality, but is a creation in the subconscious mind of the dreamer.

Following on from the above there are some people with powerful ESP who can project a visualisation-mind communication into the minds of an individual or a small group of people, transmitting an hallucination of short independent existence that appears very real to those receiving. An simile, occurs in hypnosis where in front of an audience a person who has been hypnotised is induced to see things that do not exist in reality, or conjure up an imagined past that in reality comes from a book that person has read in the past. Also, attempting to touch an Apparition will cause it to vanish. Trying to touch an Apparition projected on waking up will always cause it to disappear. Such projections are usually of someone who had died recently. (see Clairvoyance and Psychokinesis).

APPARITIONS AROUND ANCIENT BUILDINGS HISTORY SITES AND HOMES

First, we look at the science. Sites under which there is a running stream, the stream creates an electric field at right angles to the stream, some materials around this electric field are capable of absorbing the electric field and replaying the field at certain temperatures. Any incident within the site can be recorded and replayed. I can quote the science that will explain in detail how these events can happen, but this book is not the place to undertake those technicalities. One must also take into account the 'Agent', person with a telepathic ability who may be a member of a group touring areas reputed to be connected with Apparitions. An 'Agents' mind project an Apparition in the minds of others. Field trips or tours to places connected to Apparitions pose no danger to observers, because any strong-minded person can command an Apparition to desist and go away. Holding a crucifix will help but not beads, research reveals that beads will not help. More to do with tradition than anything else.

MIND TO MIND COMMUNICATION
CLAIRVOYANCE- PRECOGNITION
ARE YOU CLAIRVOYANT/ VISIONARY

These two identified categories of ESP are very real, but for all intents and purposes appear almost identical.

CLAIRVOYANCE

The gaining of knowledge over any distance-mind to mind, that could not be acquired through normal channels of information. I have outlined a test that can be used to identify people with the ESP, gifts of Clairvoyance and Precognition. People gifted with deep precognition can develop their gift to become Visionaries/ Seers.

I have researched many thousands of reports and instances of Clairvoyance/ Precognition, not to doubt that Clairvoyance is very real and lies within mind-to-mind communication, a plain of the paranormal. Statistically significant were the facts that 'sender' and 'receiver', both adults and children were related; father, mother, brother, sisters, cousins and so forth, mind to mind closeness of loved ones. Some messages were transmitted in dreams, instantaneously from faraway places such as Australia to the UK.

Normal explanations by sceptics claiming coincidence, is nonsense, because most reports were connected to a happening that **triggered** emotions, such as life-threatening accident, death of family member, a danger of significance.

Convergence – Clairvoyance - Precognition

The convergence of Clairvoyance comes into play Clairvoyants able to guess the colours on a card when the front of the card is blank. Precognition is similar but deeper; able to read complicated detailed drawings hidden from sight.

ARE YOU CLAIRVOYANT – THE TEST

This is the simple test. Gather together 10 pieces of card, plus a pen and paper on which to record results, also coloured pens or crayons. Apply the colour Red, Green, Blue, Yellow, or Black to one side of a card. Ask a friend to sit two meters away, and hold up the blank side of the card to the person being tested, who must "Call Out" the colour that comes into their mind, to the friend, who will write down the result. Ask everyone in the room to stay quiet; carry on for ten cards. Work out the percentage of calls that were correct. Those correct above fifty-fifty will give a percentage correct above spinning a coin which would be fifty-fifty. Correct calls above 50% percent correct, the result is significant, and the 'tested' is Clairvoyant. Six from 10 is 60%. Four from 10 40%. Can be improved by 15% with Meditation.

If you have this gift, you will almost certainly enjoy other abilities within the Paranormal and ESP. The gift of Precognition can be proven using the same test but substituting a drawing on the back of a card in place of a colour. Those gifted with deep Precognition can progress to becoming a Visionary/Seer.

THE ESSENCE OF MEDIUMSHIP

People gifted with ESP, particularly those gifted with Clairvoyance, can pick up echoes of the dead recorded in the minds of close relatives and friends. This can bring comfort as 'bereavement' counselling.

MEDIUMSHIP

Extensive research over the years usually concludes that Mediums claiming to speak with the dead is nothing more than a mounted show. I disagree. Whilst it is true to say that where there was money to be made in Edwardian and Victorian times, con merchants and tricksters emerged within these practices, but it would be wrong to tar modern practicians with the same brush.

I believe that genuine Mediums perform a useful role in Bereavement Counselling; helping those who cannot let go of a tragedy in their life and unable to move on. For these people a performance of talking with the dead can prevent severe trauma and nervous breakdown.

I have spoken with many Mediums who are connected to extra sensory perception, and have a natural gift of clairvoyance. A few did have multiple personalities, but this is probably a result of practicing their gift.

There are/or were one or two schools in the UK where aspiring Mediums could/can pay to be taught the techniques of controlling a mounted production in front of a paying audience.

Research around the area where production will be staged is encouraged; find out the age group of the likely audience when possible and what Christian names were popular at that time.

I will explain these major factors surrounding death and leave it to readers to make up their own mind.

It is a fact that when people die, they pass in the twinkling of an eye. Their physical body ceases and their Paranormal shadow takes over. Their complete history throughout their life is discharged on death, sending them to Reincarnation or evil people to the Unredeemed Dead for a short time, years, decades or centuries depending on the severity of their selfishness and wickedness before moving on. Nothing, yes nothing remains of that person after death except echoes in the minds of friends, relatives or loved ones. Once that person has passed, they have no memory of what went before except for some very rare cases of children remembering their past parents and where they lived.

Mediums with ESP Clairvoyance can pick up from relatives echoes of the past of deceased, but that is all. No one can speak with the deceased because their existence in the physical ceased at the point of brain death.

....

MINDFULNESS-LIVING IN THE MOMENT

Part of Meditation

Think on these things. The past is left behind. The future has not arrived. Celebrate every minute of this day by concentrating on every moment, the 'Now'. Maximise every minute of every day by suspending worries and fears; optimistic about 'the Now'. Let the past go. Forget tomorrow. Care about 'Now' because if you are not for yourself, who will be for you.

The Powers of the Universe hear your voice Now. Concentrate on the needs you have in your life for Now. Ignore any thoughts that weaken you, let them go. I repeat, give up these worries about the past. Do not worry about things that may never happen in your life. Today is Now; just enjoy and be happy in it.

The Practice

Mindfulness is part of meditation and can be practiced at any time of day or night as follows: stop thinking. Just notice everything around you wherever you are. Do not allow any thoughts to come into your mind. As thoughts appear, dismiss them, concentrate instead by looking at everything in front and around. Do not be wooden. Remain relaxed. Continue to notice everything around you whether walking, as a passenger or whatever, taking in small details- DISMISSING ANY THOUGHTS ARRIVING IN YOUR MIND.

Continue for ten minutes, increasing to twenty minutes with practice, when you are 'back in the room' after mindfulness, you will begin to feel different. All part of your advanced meditation.

THE ESSENCE OF MYSTICISM

The becoming of Mysticism follows Meditation and Mindfulness, and Mindfulness uses a sense of the presence of the Divine, a connectedness to all things at the same time remaining in the NOW. All working together to trigger the beginning of healing, followed by an intoxicated realism that, I can heal myself. I have calmed my pulse, and my blood pressure, the muscles in my neck, back and around my body achieved in just a few minutes of time. Yes, everything is becoming possible. I can cast off my old doubting self, plus continuous thoughts of an apocalyptic future. Give yourself some 'self-praise' for reaching this point.

MYSTICISM

As a world authority on the subject of Mysticism, I can reveal from my own experience that Mysticism is an important ladder by which to climb to a higher level of consciousness, and into cosmic awareness; a place where one can fly like a phoenix from the ashes of previous state of enlightenment, and leap to insights that could not have previously been achieved. A new confidence to survive whatever misfortunes come along, realising life really is an endless journey from everlasting to everlasting, along a path of cosmic truths and further enlightenment that will reveal panoramic views of the 'cosmic overturning' of all things, is underway. Plus, confirmation that the Sixth Mass Extinction of all species is gathering pace and now unstoppable, ushering in a world of change across the planet where everything will never return to the way it was. The first cosmic overturn for thousands of years, accompanied by the gross darkness of the people fetched by the Pandemic I predicted. The route into Mysticism followed by a brief look at Mindfulness, and then the practice of Scrying, whether it be by using water in a bowl or a crystal skull.

Meditation can be developed into mysticism - understanding and seeing over the heads of the crowds into a world beyond the normal. The effect for most people is reduced inhibition, plus a feeling of being in contact with Future-Time, receiving answers to questions about Future-Time, coming from outside one's normal senses.

One downside is the coming of a realisation that most people act like sheep, for example, it's okay for a stupid donkey or another animal to appear on television in an advertisement to tell viewers how and where to spend their money. Animals know better than humans? Transformation away from that level of thinking happen because Mysticism is part of the Paranormal, massless and instantaneous, from the fifth dimension to better things!

MINDFULNESS

OM MANU PADME HUM

OM MANU PADME HUM

OM MANU PADME HUM

The Prayer Wheels turning

The Chanting of a thousand Monks

Butter Lamps Burning

All is well at the Potala Palace

Thank you my friends

That strange feelings of Happiness overtook me.

MEDITATION AND PRAYER

I FOLLOW MY HEART

Here I am - THE NEW ME

My Mind is BACK HOME

I have been released from all that held me

My thoughts, emotions, hate

All flown away into a Black Hole

Never to be seen again

Follow Your Heart, My friend.

Dedicated to all who seek Happiness. The Truth is out there.
Sylvia Gladys Rayner

OUT-OF-THE-BODY
ASTRAL TRAVEL

Concentrated relaxation when the spirit splits from the physical body. I believe there is conclusive proof that part of consciousness does leave the body during operations; looking down from the ceiling in the operating theatre whilst the procedure is taking place. Consciousness splitting over a relatively short distance. When it comes to Out-of-the-Body in the form of Astral Travel, I myself travel to Tibet to walk around the village with Sun Lin and visit the studio of Alien Monk, which is very real to me personally.

Alien Monk, Sun Lin, has given to me the most accurate predictions of what is happening on our planet. This phenomenon cannot be anything other than Paranormal, when consciousness is split and separated. I believe the answer lies within the area of the phenomenon of the paranormal - instantaneous communication over any distance. This includes the necessity of my consciousness splitting and leaving my body and undergoing Astral Travel. There are many stories in the Bible of Prophets using such a phenomenon to travel instantaneously to other parts of the world. Mind is not captured in body.

....

THE ESSENCE OF PRECOGNITION
(CLAIRVOYANCE)

Extensive research over sixty years has convinced me personally that the paranormal phenomenon is very real but falls clearly into two categories.

The first is Precognition across a short distance of around 2-5 meters-mind to mind.

The second, a far more advanced Precognition, instantaneous over any distance, a shadow cast from future time, mind merging instantaneously with external fields.

PRECOGNITION
HIGHTENED AWARENESS IN CONSCIOUSNESS

My interest in heightened awareness in consciousness arose from experiments using cards with either a colour or number on one side; the card held up to an observer on the blank side, whose task it was to guess what was on the live side of the card using the Paranormal phenomenon of Clairvoyance.

Results varied, but some enthusiasts were able to achieve five to ten percent greater accuracy than the fifty percent statistic from spinning a coin. Figures from repeated tests remained about the same, sufficient to declare that there are people who are gifted with the phenomenon of Clairvoyance.

Predicting the Future

Proof is provided by an extract of my book;
ALIEN MONK
Meditation Mindfulness Mysticism Published in 2015

ISBN 9780957393998

SUN LIN SPEAKS

EARTHQUAKES, VOLCANIC ERUPTIONS, PANDEMICS, SEVERE WEATHER EVENTS SHORTAGES OF CLEAN DRINKING WATER IN SOME PARTS OF THE WORLD, WILL BECOME THE NEW REALITY

The SKULL of DOOM told you in a previous book Ronald: DARKNESS Shall Cover the Earth, and GROSS DARKNESS the peoples of the Earth. Words often repeated in your books. His reasons are simple Ronald. Movements around planet Earth of the Tectonic Plates have speeded up and there will be consequences. As for "Gross Darkness, the Peoples of the Earth". A life threatening Pandemic shall break out and spread across the World, and many people in underdeveloped countries will die, more so in under developed nations.

The more advanced form of Clairvoyance is owned by those rare individuals who can predict the future. A more complex subject, but over the years I have been able to break the phenomenon down to two clear categories:

People like myself with the brain of a code breaker, able to accurately analyse everything around at amazing speed, and come up with an answer for the future of that particular scene.

Those who again, like myself, experience a dream in technicolour of a disaster, and find that the disaster has played out in reality.

These are examples in science where human kind has observed an action, and changed its future. A clear example of the Paranormal at work.

In my first category, a man or woman with the mind of a code breaker, like myself, can look at the science, analyse every part of that scene and spot something dangerous. Give instructions to change that scene, which changes the future for that scene, and renders it safe.

My second category involves those who enjoy dreams in vivid technicolour, dreams of a disaster, and that disaster playing out in reality almost exactly as their dream.

FULL PRECOGNITION

When a disaster seen in a dream happens in reality, that is an example of the Precognition in the Paranormal - an event in Future Time coming into psychic senses today. The same considerations apply to events in Future Time seen when SCRYING.

My first example was seen whilst SCRYING with my Crystal Skull. One of my predictions published in one of my Alien Monk series of cult books, months before the event: 'An eruption of a volcano in Iceland, occurring within three days around a full moon'.

The True Story

A few months before the event, I had regular dreams in vivid technicolour, of people running with a look of terror on their faces dressed in distinct coloured jumpers, running from homes covered in a choking mist. I knew instinctively from previous experiences that this dream was predicting a happening in Future Time. I was frustrated by not recognising where this volcanic eruption was taking place until one day, a couple arrived from a Scandinavian country where they worked in the Secret Service, to chat about my role in the Independence of Ukraine, when I worked with the Ukrainian Ambassador to London; a guy in the CIA, and a Deputy Head of Ukraine KGB (recorded in my book Joseph escapes to Glastonbury 9780955790621) also to ask me for my personal assessment of the danger from Russia in the future. I told them that Russia would invade, and take control of the Black Sea Port of Ukraine under the guise of a takeover by Russian Separatists. I also told them that if we were factual and unbiased, that was where the Russian Black Sea fleet was based, and the Russians owned that area until the second world war, when it was given to Ukraine. The majority of the population in the area were Russian, and Russia will always want it back, and although I was aware that NATO was training British and Ukrainian troops in the area, Russia would never give up its former property that was necessary for housing the Russian Fleet under sole Russian control.

ICELAND

After I finished relaying my story, the male spoke up. I live in Iceland. I wear jumpers like those you describe in your dream, plus the fact that the bungalows you describe could be my parents' home. Information that enabled me to publish, in advance, my prediction that a volcanic eruption, in Iceland, would explode around three days of a full moon, months before it happened. That eruption brought air traffic in Europe to a standstill, at a cost of two billion pounds. Earthquakes will continue, but quakes that reverberate hundreds of times will culminate in a lesser volcanic eruption by releasing the forces say 5 on the scale, maximum. The next volcanic eruption that will occur, around the time of writing, will not be significant.

CONCLUSION

There are clearly two categories of Precognition. The first, a natural gift of subconsciously analysing a scene, and taking action that changes the future for that scene. Secondly, vivid dreams of an event in Future Time warning of a disaster to come. A gift that enabled small tribes of early hunter gatherers to survive and grow in number.

The second category is a natural gift of Precognition from the Paranormal - Seership and Visionary.

Having spent time as a Code Breaker, and going on to become a top Economic Forecaster, and Managing Dealer, in the City of London, I place myself in both categories.

I, Ronald Rayner, am living proof that there is a plain of Extra Sensory Perception that cast a shadow from the Future Time, into the present. I can also state that apart from personal satisfaction, there are absolutely no rewards from being either a Seer or Visionary.

....

PSYCHOKINESIS

PK can be projected by an individual over a short distance, said to be particularly strong in those going through puberty, where there is an unresolved internal phycological problem. The same psychic projections come into play by those successful at healing by laying on of hands. For me personally, I regard this phenomenon to be real, more particularly following experiments where a scientist wearing a headset linked to a small robotic vehicle were able to drive and steer the robotic vehicle by thought alone. Externalising thoughts in the brain.

Project Images
Apparitions- Poltergeists- Knocking- light bulbs exploding

THE SCIENCE My research points clearly to a discharge in the physical, of tension triggered by psychic conflict of an internal problem, proven by a human mind being capable of interfering with electrical supply, light bulbs exploding, knocking on a table; items becoming projectiles.

Personal Safety

In a strong commanding voice, tell the phenomenon to 'cease and desist immediately'. Repeat and repeat until it's gone. You personally must remain confident that you cannot be harmed by this phenomenon because its effect is over a short distance. Do not be afraid.

Some people believe that wearing a pure gold or silver cross gives them protection, and there is some evidence of the veracity of this approach. Those who have tried carrying 'worry beads' have found them not to be effective. Many apparitions are seen on waking, particularly of a loved one after their death. These are actual projections from strongly willed wish fulfilment that disappear very quickly, particularly if one talks to or tries to touch the apparition.

POSITIVE PK

The first thought that comes to mind is obvious. Mind should be able to project healing without the laying on of hands. Experiments and the result of research around the world prove that this is so. Albeit that distance appears to be a very strong factor, not working at distances beyond one to two meters. Psychokinesis is proof that good people of strong faith, when gathered together, can project a figure of Holy Mary. Proof that the paranormal plays an important part in the transmission of religious beliefs. Amen.

....

THE ESSENCE OF REINCARNATION

Following death of the biological body and brain, the essence - consciousness/soul of the deceased starts a new life in a different body, after judgement, with no memory of what went before - OR spend time with the unredeemed dead, before moving into Reincarnation.

DEATH IS PART OF PARANORMAL

Mathematicians inform us that around one hundred billion people have lived and died before us, but not one dead person has returned to life to report what happens after passing on. Quite obviously, this is because dead physical bodies cannot return, and the spirit cannot return because it has moved on.

When we die, we pass on in THE TWINKLING OF AN EYE and, when we open our eyes again, we find ourselves somewhere new, with no memory of what went before because our memory was discharged by our Paranormal Shadow at the point of brain death. We can never return to that person who previously occupied that slot in space-time.

Freezing a brain and body after a person has died in the hope that science of the future will be able to return them to life is pointless, because the essence of that person has gone in the twinkling of an eye to a new life, never to return. The very essence of that person has left their slot in space time. Mortality is programmed into every cell in our body, and is common to all life in the universe. Developments in science will be able to prolong life, but not after death. Because we go onto:

judgement/reincarnation, perhaps a time spent with the unredeemed dead. Is immutable, and will never change for time and eternity. Everything that happens in our lives, the way we lead our lives is recorded in our paranormal shadow, that is why it is very important to do harm to no one except to stop an evil act, because I promise you that act will be reflected back upon you as a bad synchronicity sometime later in your life, up until the time of death, and beyond, unless that wrong doing is repented, when it will be wiped from the record.

A history of bad things may even determine where you evolve into the next life, perhaps born to a beggar in Mogadishu, Africa. Memories in our offspring are carried forward into the next generation of our children in their genes, an essential part of survival in evolution, proving that the sins of the father shall be visited upon the children. Easily proven because drunks pass genes onto their children, leaving their children with genes sensitive to addiction.

LIFE AFTER DEATH- REINCARNATION

During my army days over half a century ago, whenever I was in danger, I used to ask myself the question 'DO I BELIEVE IN LIFE AFTER DEATH'? Sixty-five years later, I have, in my mind, as a result of continuous research over the decades accumulated an overwhelming body of evidence that tells me 'Yes'. There is definitely Reincarnation of personal consciousness that passes on into the paranormal in the 'TWINKLING OF AN EYE', after bodily death. Surprisingly for me, the overwhelming body of evidence points to a judgement on the way one has led one's life. No priest can forgive a person's sins on their death bed, because every sin must be repented by personal understanding of what was done, was wrong, and why it was wrong. There is no craftily way round the fact that every minute of every day of a person's life is recorded by their Paranormal.

People die in the twinkling of an eye, at which point the whole of their memory runs off. This is why we suddenly recall, for no apparent reason, someone met decades ago. It is a clue that the individual remembered, has died. Therefore, when people die, and Reincarnate, have no memory of the past, except in a few very rare cases, recorded in history and verified to be a fact.

The balanced and natural judgement recorded in the Paranormal determines whether that person will be reincarnated immediately or go to the Unredeemed Dead, and the gravity of the sins will determine how long an individual stays with the Unredeemed Dead (HELL).

Ten years, hundreds of years, and thousands of years of hell, and there is proof of this rule.

Speaking in tongues has been recorded by doctors and nurses caring for patients recovering from an accident or illness trauma, who wake speaking another language with no memory of their native tongue. In rare cases some of these languages have been traced back to ancient dialects or languages dating back centuries and, one case, two and a half thousand years. In the main however, most are common languages in everyday use.

The recorded cases of speaking in tongues apart from the rare frauds, are convincing stories of Reincarnation into the present life from a life lived elsewhere in the world speaking and speaking in a different tongue, and in some cases were clearly of a different sex.

This is clear evidence of a Paranormal judgement holding people in a purgatory for different periods of time, before reincarnating into their present life in present time.

FALSE CLAIMS OF REINCARNATION

My example is from the Tibetan Monasteries. Young monks in the mountainous regions of the Himalaya regularly see shining orbs floating through mountain passes. Scientists tell me that this phenomenon is balls of electrostatic electricity fetched in active areas by rocks grinding together beneath the surface. However, the creative minds amongst the elderly monks filled in their lack of knowledge about science by teaching the initiates that the orbs are the spirits of dead monks returning to their homeland. This is what they truly believe.

....

THE ESSENCE OF SCRYING
Merging of minds with external fields

Scrying is gazing into a crystal surface, or bowl of water, to seek truth by way of visions from a different plain that allows our gaze to pass through the surface into the Paranormal of Future Time. Getting to know a world outside our normal daily experience.

OR

Transmitting what we were unable to see by sight into dreams during rapid eye movement. Holding a small piece of crystal will also suffice for those who are determined to conquer the phenomenon.

SCRYING

I personally scry with the aid of crystal skulls. William Blake an eighteenth-century mystic, artist and poet, practiced scrying gazing into a bowl of water. Nostradamus practiced scrying gazing into water in a silver bowl. My personal hero, the parapsychologist, Carl Jung, practised Scrying using a Tibetan Mandala.

Whatever the method used for scrying is not really important, although I have also used the method of water in a silver bowl with some success, but with a difference. I saw nothing whilst in trance meditation gazing into a silver bowl but later, during, sleep, I experienced various scenes in bright technicolour pointing to an event in future time, all of which proved correct. The most difficult scenes to identify are earthquakes and volcanic eruptions. I clearly see earthquakes or eruptions in vivid technicolour but unless I can identify the clothes worn by the people fleeing or identify the style and design of the buildings or surrounding nature being destroyed, I am lost, until a pointer emerges during my trance meditation revealing the locations of the events. Meeting someone from Iceland enabled me to publish the prediction of the eruption in Iceland months before it occurred. All futures are coming at us every day, and every night, until they resolve into one future at the leading edge of time 'Now', although the events around which are heavily influenced by the manner in which we lead our daily life. Scrying is different. I liken it to being able to peer over the leading edge of time into future time; knowledge born in a moment of mystical insight, like access to universal knowledge.

My own personal view from my fifty years researching mysticism is that Scrying with a Crystal Skull has proved most accurate over the years, for me personally. I use three crystal skulls, all from Tibet. A typical life size crystal skull, A huge crystal skull about as much as I can lift called the 'God' skull, alleged to have been carried with the slate on which the Ten Commandments were carved, in the Ark of the Covenant.

My third crystal skull is a life size copy of an alien skull found in the Himalaya by my youngest son Craig. My favourite is a skull of an alien that fits into my hand.

Scrying is all part of Mysticism. The only ladder of which I am aware, climbs up to Cosmic Consciousness. A path of truth into an endless journey from everlasting to everlasting, a panoramic view into cosmic spirits that has convinced me that there is a life after death, and as humankind evolves, so too will the ultimate truth about the REAL GOD and REAL HOLY SPIRIT. Consciousness of which most of the world is unfamiliar, removed from normal. Mysticism is learning to relate to all states of consciousness. Being able to return to normal consciousness using what was learned at the higher level.

It is such a mistake through life to anchor one's mind in the physical world alone.

....

SYNCHRONICITY
INSTANTANEOUS MERGING WITH EXTERNAL FIELDS ACROSS TIME

A Paranormal link that fetches together incidents/events across time and space to a meaningful outcome, at a point in time; something usually beyond one's wildest imagination.

The easiest way to grasp what is a difficult concept, is for me to place before you genuine Synchronicities that have occurred in my own lifetime.

SYNCHRONICITIES

Some time ago I was filming a documentary in Jerusalem, a low-cost effort for schools, but I did not want to miss even one topographical site in the Jesus story. One area I was anxious to film was the Lithostrotos, a chapel built over the Roman pavement marked with the game of 'KING', where the Roman soldiers held Jesus, captive, whilst they played the game of 'KING' to decide who would own Jesus's one-piece garment, a much-prized treasure made in the Galilee. The Roman soldier who won the game, forced the crown of thorns onto the head of the Prophet Jesus, and forced Jesus to wear the thorns whilst carrying his Cross to Calvary, the place of Crucifixion.

Our guide told me that filming inside the Lithostrotos would not be permitted. Not taking 'no' for an answer, I went with my crew to the Chapel, knocked on the door. A polite and well-spoken Sister opened the door with a smile. I explained that I had travelled with my wife Sylvia and crew from Essex, England, specifically to film the Roman pavement on which the game of 'KING' was carved. "Essex, she exclaimed, amazing, my own sister is Principal of St Hilda School in Westcliff-on-Sea". Astonished, I told her that my late daughter Adele had attended that private school during her early school years. Furthermore, as far as I was aware, Mrs Tunnicliff was still Head and teaching at the school when we left to travel to Jerusalem." The Sister went on to name the road where she had lived with her sister as a child. My cameraman, Carl, quickly chirped up that his mother now lives in that very house. "Well, this is more than a coincidence, more like a Synchronicity", said the Sister, "and I feel privileged." "Come in, and I will give you a personal guided tour of the Chapel, the Roman pavement, and make a brief statement to your camera". We thanked the Sister, who commenced her guided tour. "The Roman paving on which the Great Prophet Jesus Stood is in the same condition today, as it was when Holy Jesus stood on the pavement two thousand year ago". Sister continued to complete a very professional piece to camera.

The mathematical odds against such a coincidence are so great that it qualifies as a Synchronicity, places in time and space, to the benefit of the documentary.

Returning to the UK after what was for me a magical trip to Jerusalem; editing footage, and applying the music to the documentary, my wife Sylvia and I, both intrigued by the piece of Calvary, given to me by sister Katarina, who attended the Altars in the Holy Sepulchre, we went in search of a modern day Urim and Thummim.

After weeks of asking questions and searching, my wife Lady Sylvia, located a small ancient box, used in early church, where it was known as the Urim and Thummim. The practice was to enter Prayer, Meditation, and choose one of the tiny scrolls, which was a key to a passage in the old or new testaments. It proved so accurate; it was scary.

ESSENCE OF TELEPATHY
MIND TO MIND COMMUNICATION
FROM FUTURE TIME

There are countless proven cases of telepathy, sufficient in numbers for me to state categorically that spontaneous paranormal occurrences are very real and, as in all Extra Sensory Perception, the door is always open to those who believe. Not believing in Telepathy may even block reception of the transmissions. Telepathy is another phenomenon proving that instantaneous transmission over any distance is real.

People gifted with a strong sense of Telepathy are often able to read from Future Time, the futures of complete strangers which just comes to them. This appears to me a specialised gift because some Clairvoyants interpret, using playing cards, very accurately in deed.

TELEPATHY
A PURE FORM OF EXTRA SENSORY PERCEPTION

Some people are receivers of information that arrives from outside their normal senses, often conveying an important message. The sender can be a relative, focusing a message to another family member. In simple terms, if someone receives a message mentally from another, the message is telepathic. Occurring more frequently between family members, irrespective of the distance apart. Here follows my personal experience of a telepathic message from my eldest son Mark. A genuine personal experience of telepathy in my own family.

LONDON/UKRAINE

I was involved in the Independence of Ukraine. Other members of the team involved were the Ukrainian Ambassador, to London, a Deputy Head of the KGB, and a CIA man. The very best intelligence service MI6, were absent because Prime Minister, Margaret Thatcher, made it very clear that she did not want the UK to be involved in the Independence of Ukraine, in spite of President Clinton needing the Independence of Ukraine to happen because Russia had five Intercontinental ballistic missile sites, housing rockets with multiple nuclear war head's that could reach the USA from

AUTHOR'S PHOTOGRAPH

The Lithostrotos - original Roman pavements where the Roman soldiers held Jesus and dressed him in a Crown of Thorns after playing the game of King. The pattern of the game is recorded on early Freemasonry badges.

Ukrainian soil. The only way the US president could get control of the missiles was for Ukraine to become Independent. Send the missile war-heads to the US, and destroy the Silos. However, it was certain that when Independence was declared, Russia would also declare the Ukrainian Rouble worthless. This problem was overcome by America agreeing to pay two billion dollars for the missile heads, when they arrived in the USA. In the meantime, Ukraine would introduce a temporary Coupon, until the US dollars arrived, when a new Ukrainian currency would be established, tied to a value for the US dollar.

Ukraine was the breadbasket to Russia. Those in charge of the Army, Navy and Air Force in Ukraine, remembered how 2m Ukrainians starved to death under Stalin. Unsurprisingly everyone cooperated, everything went well, the Independence of Ukraine was achieved, and my wife Sylvia and I were invited to Kyiv to meet other members of the original group. The CIA guy, a CIA female accountant, and a Deputy Head of the KGB, who wanted advice from me on setting up a Security Company, following Independence, to guard the large factories in Ukraine, using goods and technology from the UK.

That night, sleeping in the five-star hotel in Kyiv, I dreamt my eldest son Mark, in Ukraine, was in a box, knocking hard on the side of the box, and calling out that he wanted to talk to me urgently. I was startled to be woken at midnight when the phone rang in our room. I answered, it was the CIA man who said he was in the hotel reception and needed to talk with me urgently. He arrived in our room. I gave him coffee and biscuits. He said excitely; I have a draft drawn up President Kuchma (a close friend of President Putin), in our names, the lady accountant, your son's name, and that yourself and your wife; all listed on the 'Most Wanted Spies'. "I have sent our female to Washington to report", said the CIA man, "and I have arranged for your son to travel in the boot of a diplomat's car who will drive him to Vienna, Austria, the 'spooks' hotel, the Bristol Hotel in Vienna". We will all meet up there the day after tomorrow. It was half past midnight when I rang the KGB man and explained my problem, do not worry, I will be at your hotel sharp at 6am tomorrow morning; be ready.

True to his word, the KGB man was there outside the hotel at 6am. We stepped into his four by four and drove at over 100 kilometres an hour to the Airport, leaving our KGB tail in the dust, and took the first flight to London, from Kyiv. After arriving in London, we took the first flight to Vienna, Austria, and went straight to the Bristol hotel. I was standing outside glaring at a Russian KGB guy who had followed us when along came my eldest son Mark carrying plastic carrier bags stuffed to the brim. An hour later the CIA man arrived. What a great guy. Unprompted, he went out and bought myself and my son a white shirt, razor, soap etc, and refused to take my money. The Ukrainian KGB man sent a message that he could not make it but would meet me at the Spy Equipment shop in Mayfair, London, to arrange a large purchase of Security Goods in a weeks' time.

THE ESSENCE OF THE
UNIVERSAL COLLECTIVE SUBCONSCIOUS
A UNIFIED THEORY OF THE SUBCONSCIOUS
INSTANTANEOUSLY MERGING
WITH EXTERNAL FIELDS

Parapsychologists, and sociologists, have long claimed that the behaviour of football crowds' dates back to the tribal behaviour of early man, recorded in the Universal Collective Subconscious.

The Universal Collective Subconsciousness is another phenomenon that exists within the Paranormal - the memory of earliest tribal customs, religious beliefs, and ceremonies, plus so much more. The Paranormal records from early man, and into future time, memories of ancient UFO sightings, and alien visitations, including stone-age carvings, cave paintings, actual illustrations of UFO sightings, plus alien presence on planet Earth thousands of years in the past. Interpreted by ancient alien UFO enthusiasts as evidence worthy of deliberation.

The Universal Collective Subconscious is part of the Paranormal, and one fascinating aspect is its influence in the past, causing civilisations many thousands of miles apart to build similar structures, plus distant civilisations enjoying fundamentally similar religious rituals without any communication between those civilisations.

The Paranormal has always been a key to Evolution fetched across the planet.

....

MIRACLES IN THE PARANORMAL

THE RESURRECTION OF JESUS CHRIST WAS NOT THE TRANSFER OF A PHYSICAL BODY TO A PLACE IN SPACE THAT DOES NOT EXIST, A SCIENTIFIC INPOSSABILITY. THE TRUTH OF THE RESURRECTION IS THAT WHEN DISCIPLES SAW JESUS AFTER HIS CRUCIFIXION, THEY SAW JESUS THROUGH EXTRA SENSORY PERCEPTION IN THE PARANORMAL. THE REAURRECTION WAS VERY REAL, AND IN VERY TRUTH, AN EVENT THAT ACTUALLY TOOK PLACE IN THE PARANORMAL. JESUS, MOSES, MOHAMMED, INDEED ALL THE GREAT PROPHETS WERE IN COMMUNICATION WITH THE POWER OF THE UNIVERSE THROUGH THE REALITY OF ESP, AND NOW, FOR THE FIRST TIME IN HUMAN HISTORY, THE PARANORMAL HAS REVEALED THE FACE OF THE POWERS OF THE UNIVERSE - GOD.

After years of studying the Paranormal, Extra Sensory Perception, and Synchronicities, the very truth of the power of personal prayer, repentance, community prayers; the truth of all religious efforts stared at me from the print on the pages. The Paranormal is instantaneous communication to infinity, (any distance) to any part of the world or point in the history of the world. Religious beliefs and prayers are all very real, and true - Instantaneous Transmission to anywhere, into any time zone, Direct to GOD. Take Christianity, for example. Believers recall the stories of the Great Prophet Jesus being seen, after His Death on the Cross. Viewed through the Paranormal, this story is in very truth, and not the scientific impossibility of Reincarnating from a place that does not exist in the skies, to Earth, and Reincarnating back again after death. Jesus said that Heaven is invisible – clearly Paranormal, which solves the problem of Reincarnation for scientists. The stories of the Great Miraculous Journeys by the Great Prophet Mohammed, are all true and very real, and recorded in the Paranormal.

Also staring back at me from the pages is that no individual can forgive the sins of another, because that person has to go personally through repentance, for that sin to be remitted, and removed from their Paranormal shadow. Obviously trained Priests or Ministers of Church can provide essential guidance, and help, towards Repentance, but to hold the view that sin can be forgiven by another without personal repentance will only lead to perpetuating more sin.

PRAYER IS VITALLY IMPORTANT IN ANY RELIGION OR FAITH

People and communities are not wasting their time when they pray, because Prayer and Repentance travel instantaneously across time and space to the Powers of the Universe, GOD, whether sent from the privacy of one's own bedroom, or a place celebrating belief. Prayer and Repentance are never a waste of time. However, always remember that when asking for something in prayer, the system requires you to do everything in your own power first to achieve what is wanted, because prayer is asking for that little bit extra, albeit through the Paranormal, to fetch perhaps a Synchronicity to solve a problem.

It has taken centuries for the mind of modern man to understand the very truth of the Resurrection, and similar important events or happenings across various religions. Early writers of religious texts were aware that a mysterious force pervading what they were doing, but were unaware that it was in the Paranormal.

The Paranormal is also proof that religious conversions in all Religions, and Belief Systems, recorded in history over the centuries, were all very REAL, AND TRUE, A REVELATION FROM GOD, only now released in the year 2021.

PROOF THAT PRAYER WORKS

MIRACLES RECORDED IN THE CHRISTIAN BIBLES AND OTHER HOLY TEXT SUCH AS IN THE HOLY KORAN, THE SACRED BOOK OF ISLAM, FOR EXAMPLE, DICTATED TO MOHAMMED BY THE ANGEL GABRIEL, ARE PROVEN TO BE TRUE BY THE PARANORMAL

THIS UNDERSTANDING WILL, OVER TIME, CHANGE AND REINFORCE THE FACE OF RELIGIONS, BY GIVING RELIGIOUS TEXTS ABSOLUTE CREDABILITY ACROSS THE PLANET. GOD, THE POWER OF THE UNIVERSE, HAS REVEALED FOR THE FIRST TIME IN RELIGIOUS HISTORY, IN THIS BOOK, A FACE TO THE WORLD. HOW TO COMMUNICATE DIRECTLY THROUGH PRAYER, AND THE TERMS UNDER WHICH THE LINE WILL BE CONNECTED, AS LAID DOWN BY THE PROPHETS - THE VERY FIRST COMMANDMENT OF WHICH IS IMMUTABLE - 'THOU SHALL NOT KILL'.

THIS NEW REVELATION REINFORCES IN 2021, THAT COMMUNICATION WITH THE POWERS OF THE UNIVERSE, THROUGH PARANORMAL, IS OPEN EQUALLY TO BOTH MALE, AND FEMALE, AND CHILDREN ALIKE; OF ANY RACE, OR COLOUR, OR RELIGIOUS FAITH - ALL ARE EQUAL BEFORE THE POWERS OF THE UNIVERSE- GOD, AND ANYONE, YES ANYONE, WHO CLAIMS TO SPEAK FOR GOD MUST THEMSELVES BE HUMANLY PERFECT, AND WILL BE JUDGED FAR MORE SEVERELY THAN ANY OTHERS FOR ANY WRONG DOING. WHAT THEY DO NOT HAVE, IS THE AUTHORITY TO ADD TO OR TAKE AWAY ANYTHING FROM GOD'S COMMANDMENTS OR HIS MANY PROPHETS. ONLY GENUINE PERSONAL REPENTENCE WILL FORGIVE SIN AND FETCH FORGIVENESS - SO HELP ME GOD.

....

GOD SPEAKS

I delight in everything I write because everything I write is true, to the best of my knowledge.

The heading, 'God Speaks'. God has spoken to me during my lifetime but only rarely, and not in a loud voice. I will explain my experiences of God communicating with me directly, that led to the texts in this book.

I am eighty-three years old at the time of writing and recently, late in the evening, I was practicing squats, because 'if you don't use it you will lose it'. I lost my balance whilst straightening up, fell backwards and cracked the back of my head heavily on a brick fireplace. I think I felt unconscious with pins and needles in my arms, but with the help of my wife Sylvia, pulled myself up into a wide leather armchair. Dazed, I was discussing with my wife the need to call a paramedic to check me out. We weighted this against the prospect of lying in a hospital bed over the weekend, and catching the Corona virus.

Around an hour later I was standing steadily, no shakes, with my arms outstretched. There was a large egg size swelling on the back of my head, plus blood. I said my prayers before getting into bed, holding my piece of Calvary given to me by Sister Katarina who tended the Three Altars in the Holy Sepulchre in Jerusalem, while I was filming there. Next morning, I awoke. No sign of any swelling on my head or broken skin. I felt great, as though my accident had never happened.

A little later when I was preparing my days clothes, I felt overwhelmed with elation. A voice came into my head, 'how sweet Thou art Ronald, how sweet thou art'. It took me a few days to get over the overwhelming sensation, because I knew it was the Voice of God. A voice and feeling I had experienced previously on the rare occasion when God communicated with me directly. Harking back to that experience of Sylvia with our crew filming in Jerusalem. We found it difficult to get permission to film in the Holy Sepulchre. The break-through came when an influential Muslim Guard said he would take us into the Sepulchre for five hundred dollars, at six am, next morning.

When we arrived with our Camera Man, and Sound Recordist, we found a solitary Nun, Sister Katarina, wearing carpet slippers to keep her feet warm, kneeling on the floor, cleaning the base of the Cross of Crucifixion, where the base of the cross went into the rock of Calvary. Sylvia and I took turns holding her hands to keep her warm. Katarina told her story to camera. She was laying in her bed in California USA, close to death, when she saw an Apparition of Holy Mary who spoke to her, 'Katarina, you will not die, in future you will be serving in the Old City of Jerusalem, where Jesus was Crucified'.

Katarina arrived as the Commandoes from Israel drove the Muslim guards from the area of the three Altars. Katarina cleaned the surface around the indentation in the rock where the cross entered. This was to be covered in protective glass. Katrina showed me three very small pieces of rock held in her hand, "These came away in my hand as I cleaned, and I carry these with me always, but I am giving them to you Ronald. A gift from God that will enable you to, See The Future". That was the point at which I fully developed my ability as a Visionary. Unfortunately, modern human beings are so arrogant, and full of themselves; many ignorant, they are not going to listen to anyone. I have found this to be the case over the past ten years, in spite of my one hundred per cent accuracy in my predictions.

The Voice of God and the Hand of God, guided me in writing this book. The purpose of which is to reveal to everyone everywhere, in any religion or belief system across the world – Prayer whether from a man, woman, child, or group, is communicated instantaneously to the Powers of the Universe – God. And to reinforce Gods Commandment – "Thou Shalt Not Kill", and for anyone to tell another, you can kill in God's Name is the greatest abomination to Almighty God.

CONNECTING WITH THE HOLY SPIRIT THROUGH THE PARANORMAL

I can do this, and this phenomenon has revealed itself to me in simple ways. For example, if something important occupies my prayers, just before I receive a positive happening, in the physical world, my mind is taken over with Hymns I PERSONALLY sing regularly. Occupying my mind for one or two hours. If I do something that is right, and good, the following morning my head is pervaded with Hymns, or a single Hymn, and I know that I have received a message from the Holy Spirit through the Paranormal - all part of The Face of God, and The Nature of God; 'Be Glad'.

PARANORMAL ALIEN ABDUCTIONS

The Drake Equation calculates from its five-piece equation that there are 10,000 civilisations in our Galaxy within the Milky Way. Drake is a fascinating equation, devised by world leading scientists, and should be taken seriously because evolution dictates that intelligence is an integral part of evolution, and will arise anywhere and everywhere. Little wonder, therefore, that alien UFOs have been seen gracing Earths skies, but why 'the big silence' with SETI listening twenty-four seven. Fifty years of searching has not found one signal from any civilisation out there amongst countless billions of stars. However, the absence of an alien signal does not deny that alien UFO are in Earths skies. SETI must be given extended funding to widen their search in the light of the latest technological discoveries

PARANORMAL ALIEN ABDUCTIONS RESEARCH INDICATES THAT SIGHTINGS OF GENUINE ALIEN UFOS ARE REAL, BUT VERY RARE.

ARE THEY INVOLVED IN ALIEN ABDUCTIONS IN THE PARANORMAL.

There is more than sufficient reliable evidence from pilots of military aircraft, plus experienced airline pilots, both of whom can give reliable descriptions of what they have seen, to know that sightings of genuine alien UFOs are very real but very rare.

Alien UFOs have been seen more frequently in Earths skies since the 1940's, when the term UFO was born. High ranking government ministers from across the world have added their voices to the fact of alien UFOs being a reality. Excellent men, such as a former Canadian Minister of Defence, has been urging governments to admit to the general public that Alien UFOs are very real, and are an on-going phenomenon. If we delve back into history, numerous drawings, paintings and carvings over centuries, point to Alien UFOs in our skies. In the present day, Alien UFOs are seen travelling across our solar system at great speed without stopping, by professional Astronomers. Such craft are most likely to be the origin of an alien signal; transmitting as it goes, but will be lost when the craft leaves the solar system. Some could be 'Star ships' that have been travelling for a very long time indeed.

The main categories of UFO fall into cigar shape, triangular, or saucer shaped craft that can slow, hover, and dart away at great speed at acute angles, the 'G' forces of which would kill any humanoid pilot, which tells us immediately that the UFOs are either unmanned or piloted by robots. Movements that are not too difficult to accomplish when one watches a dragon fly chasing food. To imitate the abilities of a dragonfly it is a matter of being able to manoeuvre 360 degrees, instantaneously.

Most sightings of UFOs purported to be of Alien origin are not Alien UFOs.

Probably as high as ninety seven percent of alleged Alien UFO sightings by members of the general public are not alien UFOs, but can eventually be explained away as unusual weather phenomena, ball lightning, balls of electrostatic charge created by movement of underground rocks; controlled drones and other astrophysical phenomena. It is highly probable that genuine Alien UFO in our skies, hovering or landing, are simple exploring our Blue planet; as we on Earth are exploring planet Mars. Albeit that governments are powerless to stop them. To undertake complicated measures, those saucers or landers would need to be controlled by robots. Does that make any difference? Yes. The craft would be capable of abducting people, and taking samples from animals, all very dangerous because of the possibility of cross contamination from Alien bacteria, to which earthlings would have no immunity. Any Alien Abduction should be of international importance. However, many Governments would necessarily cover up such events by pretending there are no such things as Alien UFOs. It is difficult to separate out the truth of alleged Alien Abductions when governments muddy the waters by insisting that no Alien UFO has landed on Earth, and that no Alien Abductions has ever occurred, albeit that Governments have no idea about the reality of Alien Abductions in the Paranormal. The two most likely credible reasons for alien abductions are; to renew human DNA that will grow weaker in Alien Nations using Cyborgs. Secondly, to breed a human hybrid that could survive on planet Earth.

Most abductions are reported in America, but that makes sense to me because any Alien nation looking in on planet Earth would head to the most powerful economy and military resources on Earth - America.

The idea that Aliens may be living somewhere on planet Earth when hundreds of Astronomers, Astrophysics and the International Space Station are continually watching the skies is a step too far. Nevertheless, stories that UFOs have been seen by naval personnel disappearing into lakes and oceans persist. This could be a reality if an Alien Star Ship were cloaked somewhere in our Solar System to which such craft would return. To be capable of such technology, and intelligence would be multiple log scale greater than the intelligence of Earthlings. Such a scenario would indeed make the harvesting of DNA by Aliens feasible. There is also the possibility of Aliens making use of Paranormal to interfere on planet Earth.

TIME TO EXPLOIT COMPLETELY NEW IDEAS OF COMMUNICATING WITH ALIENS

After drawing a blank for so many years, it is time for Clairvoyant groups to come together and come up with a completely new approach and new ideas for providing a channel for communications with Aliens. Humans capable of receiving messages outside normal channels; through the Paranormal. Clairvoyants, for example, is probably the best place to start. Programme Makers, indeed all Aliens enthusiasts must apply new ways of thinking to revealing Alien interference on planet Earth.

Paranormal Groups, meeting together, must not have anyone present in the room who shows the slightest scepticism towards the subject. Neither can communicating by rapping be allowed, because it is open to simple fraud.

Groups must persevere and avoid changes in group members until a new project commences. I do not pretend that it will not be difficult for the most experienced Clairvoyants to interpret any signal or messages because we have no idea whatsoever of what form Alien communication will take; symbols, maths or whatever. Groups must write down and record everything that comes into their minds; complex signs or any star pattern, anything mathematical, drawings, geometrical, noise patterns, invitation to a certain place. Sketch any Apparition that come into mind. Write details of any paranormal event such as splitting consciousness, looking down on the room.

IMPORTANT NOTE

If any member finds that an echo from an earthly spirit is trying to break through, listen carefully because that communication may have suffered an Alien Abduction, in which case make careful notes. If, however, it an echo of a nuisance spirit keeps interfering, stand up and say firmly; BE GONE Earthly Spirit, this place is not for you.

If and when any intelligible message is recorded, it is your duty to inform the national press, radio and television stations of the facts. Witness support will be very important.

A PRELIMINARY TO ALIEN ABDUCTION
IN THE PARANORMAL

POTENTIAL ADVANCED WARNING ABOUT POSSIBLE FUTURE DANGER FROM AN ALIEN SOURCE

Governments across the world must take seriously stories about actual physical Alien Abductions and particularly Alien Abductions in the Paranormal; where the abductee has not moved from their bed. Significance should be attached to sightings of an Alien UFO by a Clairvoyant before either form of abduction has taken place.

We, on Earth, are only around three million years old since the early primates started eating meat triggering the birth of babies with enlarged brains. Theoretically, the evolution of the human race has now reached a dead-end, that is until advances in technology came along and gave human being unlimited external brain power through computerisation. Previously the size of the human brain was at 'stop', because it is as large as a human heart pumping blood circulation around the body can manage. Human life is facing a dead end as overpopulation fetches global warming followed by a mass extinction, but technology and reduced numbers will help human populations survive until the next Ice Age, when the Earth is refreshed and starts again. Nevertheless, the tendency is towards the loss of the most valuable element in the universe - human DNA. This tragedy will have struck alien civilisations across the Universe, particularly those that have developed indestructible self-repairing robots, and uploaded their minds into these robots to become immortal Cyborgs; a further loss of human line DNA.

To reach planet Earth, crossing the vast distances involved, Alien civilisations will need to be far advanced than the primitive humans on planet Earth; who fight and destroy whole Towns and Villages communities over small religious differences. Aliens who need to replenish human DNA will plan very sophisticated exploration of planet Earth: prepare everything very carefully over a period of time. Alien abductions in the Paranormal could be the start of preparations of an Alien plan to harvest human DNA from planet Earth, posing the question; are we on planet Earth receiving a warning from Future Time of Paranormal events that have started to arrive from Future Time via the Fifth Dimension? Are Aliens interfering on planet Earth?

SCAREY PARANORMAL

There are literally thousands of cases, more particularly in the USA, where people are convinced that they have been abducted by Aliens, and are suffering all the disorientating after effects to the point where they need after-care, albeit that they have never left their bed. Nothing, apparently, will persuade these abductees otherwise, because they can describe in detail every stage of their abductions; the interior of an alien space ship, (primitive) medical type tests carried out on their bodies. It is reported that the psychological effect on abductees is so severe, many of the alleged Abductees requiring after care by a trained Psychologist. The important missing link in these stories is that neither the authorities or the abductees are aware that their abduction took place in the Paranormal. Their abductions were very real in every respect outside the physical, raising a very serious and profound question to world governments.

1. HOW MANY OF THE CLAIMED ALIEN ABDUCTIONS FOLLOW SIGHTINGS BY ABDUCTEES OF AN ALIEN UFO.

2. HOW MANY OF THE ABDUCTEES SUFFER THE BRIGHT LIGHT PHENOMENON ENABLING ALIENS TO TAKE CONTROL OF THEIR MENTAL PROCESSES THROUGHOUT THEIR ABDUCTION.

3. ARE THESE TECHNOLOGIES CLEARLY BEYOND THE UNDERSTANDING OF EARTHS SCIENTISTS.

4. IS THERE THE REMOTEST POSSIBILITY THAT- ABDUCTIONS IN THE PARANORMAL ARE DRIVEN BY ALIEN UFO/S 'CLOAKED' SOMEWHERE ON EARTH OR IN EARTH'S ATMOSPHERE.

5. IS THERE AN ALTERNATIVE POSSABILITY - A SHADOW FROM FUTURE TIME, PLAYING OUT EVENTS FROM FUTURE TIME, IN THE PARANORMAL, AS A WARNING OF UP-COMING EVENT.

6. ARE THERE PARALLEL REALITIES EXISTING SIMULTANEOUSLY, INCLUDING THE UNIVERSAL COLLECTIVE SUBCONSCIOUS OF PAST, PRESENT, AND FUTURE TIME, EXISTING TOGETHER OUTSIDE SPACE-TIME. [In My House there are many mansions]

WE NEED TO KNOW

My findings are a wake-up call to all professional UFO investigators, scientific investigations of the UFO phenomenon, and Programme Makers of UFO material; to cast off the old, and look at the new face of an Alien Phenomenon. Are Aliens projecting into planet Earth, perhaps understanding Earthlings are blind to the Paranormal, a super shadow OVER every human, of such complexity, instantaneously connected everywhere across planet Earth, and communicating the Paranormal, Extra Sensory Perception, and Synchronicity; the final step in the completion of the evolving of human kind. A sophisticate that carries higher intelligence into that which some can tap and hear the powers of the universe – HEARING GOD, think?

EVERY HABITABLE PLANET HAS A BIOSIS

The biosphere of every habitable planet has a biosis that forms a cybernetic wave that flows across the Universe. An instantaneous physiological intelligence of every habitable planet. It is the Super Organism responsible for communicating the Paranormal, Extra Sensory Perception and Mysticism. The force that pervades every habitable planet, so massive, so complex, interconnected everywhere across the solar system. A cybernetic that transcends humanity and planets. Part of the continuous development of evolution on every habitable planet in the Universe. A wave flowing instantaneously across our Universe.

VISITING SUN LIN - ALIEN MONK
Out of the body

I walked into my garden, set up my Crystal Skull on a small antique table beside my chair, with Wilson, my skeleton, sat alongside in his Tibetan costume. I offered a Crystal Skull to the North, South, East and West. Said the Lord's Prayer for protection, holding my piece of Calvary from the Altar of Crucifixion in the Holy Sepulchre in Jerusalem, given to me by sister Katarina who tended that altar, as a gift to me whilst I was filming my documentary Jerusalem. I sat in my chair and went into trance Meditation, but nothing happened over two days, I felt concerned that I had 'lost it', but the third day, success.

I found myself sitting in Sun Lin's studio in Tibet. I have greatly missed our talks Sun Lin "And I you Ronald". "FIRST RONALD, ALLOW ME TO CONGRATULATE YOU ON BEING THE FIRST VISIONARY TO PREDICT THE COMING OF THE WORLDWIDE PANDEMIC AND THE DEVASTATION IT WILL CAUSE IN UNDERDEVELOPED COUNTRIES WHO CANNOT AFFORD THE VACCINE".

Sun Lin, I am writing my most difficult book yet, explaining in detail of the amazing Paranormal Phenomena communicated to me directly by God.

"Ronald, you and I are both aware that the understanding of the workings of the universe will never be complete unless and until there is realisation that the Paranormal is a plain IN ITS OWN REALITY where communication is instantaneous over any distance. The Paranormal is not in the physical world, but influences everything in the physical world, Ronald"

The Paranormal drove evolution, giving early humanoids the ability to copy and innovate, driving improvement in human intelligence separating humans from animals, to the extent that every human has a Paranormal shadow that leaves the body at the point of death, after dispersing the history of every minute of every day of that human life, which forms the Judgement. The Paranormal Shadow does not connect to birth until a child's mind becomes aware, 'I think therefore I am'. I am sitting here looking out - a child's earliest memory.

Eventually Ronald, general awareness of the Paranormal, will fetch great changes across the planet. Human behaviour everywhere will change across the world, like the changes fetched by the Pandemic you predicted in your books following my counselling, Ronald.

'Darkness shall cover the Earth and gross darkness the people of the Earth', was the warning we gave to mankind Ronald'. A warning that fell on deaf ears, as I anticipated.

The Secrets Of Tibetan Tea

I had been anticipating your arrival Ronald, and I have made a mug of your favourite Tibetan tea, the ingredients of which is a chip from a three-kilo block of tea from China. I believe that is where the saying in your country, 'a chip off the old block' originated, Ronald.

Please describe to me once again Sun Lin how you arrive at this delicious brew. I, personally Ronald, carry a pouch of roasted barley with me, being always prepared for any tea events in the Monastery. We used to pour the tea through a strainer into a wooden cylindrical churn, where it is mixed with yak butter, soda, and salt. After vigorous churning with the wooden plunger the liquid takes on the quality of a soup, when it is poured into a teapot and left standing to brew on a hot plate until required. I mix my roasted barley with the tea which gives a more pronounced flavour and substance. I confess Sun Lin that the flavour from a mug of your tea is richer, and tastier than village tea. The villagers have easy access to walnuts Ronald, but roasted barley is increasingly more expensive. However, since the Chinese have taken control, I do see village children eating bananas and other snacks with their tea, luxuries they have never enjoyed in the past.

Sun Lin, I have thought long and hard about the philosophy of the Tibetan plateau, and the villages around Monasteries. The women of the villages suffered one of the worst mortality rates during birth, and the mortality of newly born was amongst the highest in the world. Monks walked through the town and villages begging rice and food from people who barely had sufficient food for themselves.

I put it to you Sun Lin that these Monks, and Initiates, hundreds of men young and old should have been working in the fields to produce enough food for everyone, plus a surplus to raise money for medical equipment and professional midwives, rather than spending every day sitting in a Monastery cross legged Chanting, Meditating, and Debating, producing absolutely nothing towards the local and regional economy.

Ronald, I agree with you wholeheartedly. Everything in the past was captured in ignorance due to self-isolation and lack of knowledge of the latest scientific developments.

Things are different now Ronald, since the Chinese have taken control. There are doctors, midwives, nurses and access to hospitals. Against that, street and stone signage, are in Chinese Mandarin. Only in the Tibetan Autonomous Regions are Tibetans allowed to speak their language without having to make a trip to a police station. Perhaps the most startling development is that young male Tibetans are no longer signing to join Monasteries, preferring instead the bright lights, popular music, and promiscuity. Young Chinese appear to have much less grasp on the principles of morality than young Tibetans.

The last time we met Ronald, I reported that young initiates in the Monastery were disobeying the instructions from their Master, preferring to disappear away from their Monastery at weekends to enjoy what they describe as the good life. Rumour has it that less than five hundred are joining Monasteries across Tibet. In my opinion Ronald, this is not a bad development, because Tibet has remained captured far too long in ignorance, superstition, and too many mothers and babies dying in childbirth.

The Chinese have educated Tibetans to Medicine, and leading a purposeful life by using their talents to the full. That said, Tibet is potentially one of the most attractive tourist destinations in the world, the 'Pearl of Great Price'. It would be wrong of the Chinese to discourage tourists from around the world to visit Tibet, for its uniqueness alone, Sun Lin.

There is no doubt in my mind that very quickly all Tibetans including far Western Tibet will become 'Chinesed'. Portraits of the Dalai Lama are prohibited, and even those hidden by the old faithful will disappear as the whole of Tibet becomes China. Doubtless tiny pockets of devout Tibetans, and Muslims will go underground, but in the longer term they will never outwit the Chinese police.

In the days when Tibet was isolated, young men spending their lives sitting cross legged, in Monasteries, chanting, to become enlightened, is in truth a nonsense of the undeveloped uneducated mind, living isolation from the outside world away from latest scientific and other developments. When I was a young Monk in Lhasa Ronald, visiting Chinese were rare, but always easy to spot because they usually wore shoes with no heels made from a black cloth. Chinese travelling salesmen and visitors always drank green tea without milk, in preference to nourishing Tibetan Tea. Visiting Chinese Taylors would measure customers with a piece of string, marking the cloth with powered chalk, cutting the garment from the cloth on the spot, in front of an audience of onlookers amazed at the skill and speed of the Chinese garment maker. Sometimes the payment was by barter, unlike the present day when the coming of the Chinese has made many luxuries available to anyone who has the money to pay.

We should never forget the Tibetan Monks in their Monasteries have given to the world gems of un-calculable value, for easing the strains of modern society across the world:

Meditation
Mindfulness
Mysticism
Routes into the Paranormal

The very practice of becoming isolated from other societies, and the world; sitting all day, every day, of their God given life in a Monastery, is proof in itself that their minds were not developing fully, other than in a very narrow specialised way, as in many ancient religious societies, believing that enlightenment is inexpressible, and cannot be explained in words, which is completely untrue. Meditation can be explained in words, so too the gaining of experience of Mindfulness and Mysticism.

We die, in the twinkling of an eye, the next time we open our eyes into our new reality we will have no memory whatsoever of what was before. We are born new again. Whether anyone will be happier or better is determined by the manner in which they lived their last life. Put simply, anyone who was a wicked person, could be born a beggar in Mogadishu, Africa. Sitting cross legged in a Monastery chanting and finding enlightenment without the effort of bringing up children, the worry of getting to work on time, paying the bills, walking and driving in noise and pollution, fear of being stabbed by an underprivileged youth in a police-less society; scrounging food from the less well off - great if you can get it, but is not the way into total enlightenment. To see truth, we need to live and see the world around us. Living in isolation means being left behind by natural evolution, being kept behind with a backward idea of reality.

THE HERMIT

High above the Himalaya

High above the Sea of Time

The girl sat suspended

The Sun The Moon The Stars

Her home for evermore

THE SPHERES

The Balls of Light

The Spheres of the Cosmos

Travelled at speed

Gathered around her

Whispering the sweet language of Love

On a journey of unknown beauty

THE HERMET

They call her The Hermit

Living far above the clouds

Surrounded by darkness

Her life of Meditation and Prayer

Beyond our dreams

THE RAVEN

But wait my friend

Do you see the Shadow

The Spirit of the Raven

Watching over her

The black wings stretched out in flight

Waiting for her Midnight Prayer

The Prayer of the Buddha

THE VOICE

My body is like a Mountain

My eyes are like the Ocean

My mind is like the Sky

THE JOURNEY

Slowly his wings beat the air

Their eyes met

She softly touched him

Mystical Powers began to rise

Swirling as the glow of the Mandala

Filled the darkness

Once again He Took Her

On a Spiritual Journey

The Spheres softly singing

As they entered the Enchanted Gardens

Soothing the Lamas with sweet smelling herbs

The Potala Palace

Glowed with a thousand Butter Lamps

The Chanting rising to a Heavenly Embrace

Thank You My Sweet Friend

THE SPELL

Tears came

Then the Laughter

Her Eyes as a thousand Stars

Lost in the spell

As she gazed into the darkness

Into the night

The Power of the Universe

Once more watched over her

The Hermit dedicated to our friend Alexandra David-Neel

Sylvia Gladys Rayner

And every Space that a Man views around his dwelling-place
Standing on his own roof or in his garden on a mount
Of twenty five cubits in height, such space is his Universe
And on its verge the Sun rises, and sets, the Clouds bow
To meet the flat Earth and the Sea in such an ordered Space
The starry Heavens reach no further, but here bend and set
On all sides and the two Poles turn on their Valves of gold
And if he moves his dwelling place his Heavens also move
Where'er he goes, and all his neighbourhood bewail his loss
Such are the Spaces called Earth and such its dimension.

William Blake

TRACEY FLETCHER -
PROFESSIONAL CLAIRVOYANT AND MYSTIC –
UFOs AND ALIEN ABDUCTION

Tracey Fletcher, a long experienced professional Clairvoyant and Mystic, tells her story, in her own words, of seeing a UFO, followed shortly after by her Abduction in the Paranormal. An event that has affected Tracey for the rest of her life.

My name is Tracey Fletcher, and I was born at home in 1963 in West Ham in East London, England, but I grew up in Dagenham, Essex, England. Whilst growing up I enjoyed varied interests in my life, and was a happy healthy teenager. My secret to a happy life were music, gymnastics, and dancing.

One evening in 1979, something quite extraordinary happened that would remain with me for the rest of my life. In the April I turned sixteen, and was in my final year at school. The school was Parsloes Manor Comprehensive, which was attached to a big park called Parsloes Park. One evening after leaving my boyfriend's house sited behind the park, I had a strange experience. My boyfriend at the time would walk me to the edge of the park, and I walked on further to my home by myself in ten minutes. On one particular evening on my journey home across the park, the stars were out enabling me to see because it was not total darkness. The time was around 9.50 pm, and the weather was dry. I remember it was mid-year and I needed to be home by 10pm; very fit I was walking a fast pace. I passed my school to my left. In front of me was a lit-up Avenue a few hundred feet from the road. I started to feel a heavy presence above my head. I became very dark, and I felt like ducking down whilst walking. I did not feel right, and stopped in my tracks. I looked up and saw the biggest, blackest, UFO above my head. It made no sound on its approach; it was just there. It must have been high up but it was enormous in size. It was saucer shaped, metallic black, with a circular section underneath. The diameter of that section alone seemed to me to be around one hundred feet. I looked down shaking my head in disbelief. Looking up it was still there. I just stared at the UFO, and felt that I could not move. It hovered over me for what appeared to me to be seconds. I was truly transfixed to the spot. In our time, it felt like a minute at least, before it started rising upwards. Then it tilted to one side, with the underneath towards me which enabled me to see what appeared to be hundreds of lights. It was not of this world. It was magnificent. It suddenly flew away at what appeared to be something like the speed of light, juddered, the clouds split and it appeared to move into another dimension. I was totally blown away. I saw starlight again as it tilted to fly off with the effect of leaving the rest of the park blacked out.

I began running home in a state of shock, reaching my house within five minutes. I banged on the front door in a state of hysteria, blurting out to my mother and two brothers what I had just seen. My mother gave me a blank look and commented that it was getting late. It was obvious to me that they did not know what to believe.

The next day I checked the newspapers, and there had been some other sightings of UFOs across the country. I was bewildered, and did not know what to do in so far as reporting my own personal experience to the press, or whoever. My mother gave me no guidance, and I did not report the event to anyone.

I borrowed some books from the library to ascertain whether or not I could find anything in the Paranormal sections that would give me some answers. At that time, I was not even aware UFOs existed. I, nevertheless, had my first close encounter of the First Kind. One evening three weeks later I went to bed in my small box-room, at the front of the house, and I slept facing the window. This particular night, I saw the UFO I had encountered three weeks previously hovering above the roof of the house, and I saw clearly the black circular section underneath the UFO. My first thought was, how am I going to pass through the ceiling.

When suddenly I felt myself being levitated through the ceiling and through the circular section beneath the UFO. I could not see anyone, no entities, nevertheless it felt distinctly that there was a presence, but I cannot recall whether I was sitting or standing. What I could see were advanced computer screens appearing to be just sitting transparently in space, playing light sequences continuously. I was staring at the computer screen for what appeared to be ages.

Nothing else was happening although I felt that I was being spoken to telepathically. I remember thinking, 'what does all this mean'. I recall I was looking to my right, and I was told to look to my left; another screen, and sequencies of lights. I sensed one single entity was communicating with me telepathically, but I could not see anyone. I felt I was being shown information about existence; some sort of download that continued all night. At no time did I feel uncomfortable, before being returned to my bed in the house. Next morning when I awoke, I was the wrong way round in my bed, and my duvet and covers were around six feet way across the room close to my bedroom door, all very strange.

*Aristocratic Tibetan Woman from Shigatse
wearing regional costume and
carrying a hunting purse with bullets.*

I remembered the dream vividly. It seemed so real. After some time, I developed a strange rash on my left arm, that appeared to me like fibres under the skin spreading out gradually, hence I visited my doctor who said, 'it was not like anything he had ever seen', and he was for nearly all my life, but has not troubled me. I decided to put up with it. Over forty-one years later the malady is barely visible. I may have told the doctor at the time that I saw a UFO, but clearly, he did not know what to think about my explanation of the problem on my arm.

Following my seeing the UFO I am convinced that it helped me to develop an exceedingly good reading capacity. I have read books from a young age, but now I am reading a book a day, concentrating particularly on books about the paranormal. This speciality necessitated my visiting a 'cult' book shop in Shaftesbury Avenue in the West-End of London, because local libraries were unable to stock my specialised choice of books.

I noticed over time I was developing an advanced awareness of everything, psychic and telepathic in my daily life. At sixteen years of age, I started a job in London with the Tanzanian Government as a diamond sorter, in spare time training in martial arts, in Shaolin and Kung Fu, Wing Chun. I learnt Meditation at the age of nineteen with a guru, MAHARAJI-JI which opened up my awareness of my 'third eye', when I started to see things from different perspectives. Life was good because I was manifesting everything I wanted to be and become.

I met a woman from South Africa who was a true Mystic, and twelve years older than myself. She taught me about magic in the eastern world, Mysticism, the importance of the works of Carl Jung, LAO - TZU, Taoism, so many and varied subjects. Strangely, as I mastered these subjects, I felt instinctively that they made perfect sense, and I felt that I knew part of their magic already, because everything fitted into a pattern. Many Synchronicities have occurred in my lifetime, too many to mention, but sufficient to erase any doubts in my mind about the subject.

As a Clairvoyant, I predict things regularly, when I think about certain persons who are able to call me or find me after years of losing contact with them. When I was twenty years old, I was on a ferry boat crossing the sea in mid-winter, laying on a large sofa half-awake trying to get to sleep. Suddenly I visioned and felt myself flying across the sea to my home in England. I gazed at my flat, at the windows which were open, and exuding steam. It was snowing and I wondered why my boyfriend had left the windows open. I then fell into sleep. A few hours later I reached my home town when I remembered my Astral travel. Looking up at the windows of my house, they were open and steam issuing from them. A true out-of-the-body experience, that convinced me Astral travel is true.

Between 2015-2017 I was witnessing some strange phenomenon is the skies between around 11pm and 1am, when I was out walking with my dogs. Standing on a hill in the park, from behind me came a massive very bright object moving slowly, the width and length of which is comparable with a motorway, then moving off at a rapid speed. Another evening I saw a golden bright arrow moving into the only cloud in the sky before disappearing. On occasions I could see stars suddenly start to move and change direction, or follow a zig zag pattern. All my sightings were in Essex, England, United Kingdom.

My whole life feels like it has thrown me from one mission to the next. Nevertheless, I am very grateful for my enhanced gifts, revealing a world full of wonders, including the Synchronicity that brought me to the author of this book, and the opportunity to tell my stories plus amazing personal experiences that I hope will encourage others not to be afraid to come forward and reveal what has happen to them.   **Tracey Fletcher.**

Analysis of Tracey Fletchers UFO sighting and Alien Abduction

Tracey Fletchers story is previously unpublished, but is important because it shines a light on the phenomenon of an experienced and professional Clairvoyant seeing an alien UFO, and shortly afterwards experiencing an Alien Abduction, in either the physical or Paranormal, which opens the door to a wholly different view of the Alien phenomenon – dangerous with long lasting effect – pointing to the possibility that people with Clairvoyant ability are more likely than others to see UFOs, and suffer Alien Abductions? Is this experience, in reality, being captured temporarily in another dimension or a mysterious alien force able to imitate or manipulate the Paranormal? OR Is it a phenomenon from future time manipulated by mysterious Alien forces that pose a possible danger to the population on planet Earth in Future Time?

There have been many cases from across the world of abductees being left with some physical effect on one or both arms which makes Tracey's case very important in scientific terms, because there has to have been some kind of force field projected from outside Tracey's home to achieve an Alien Abduction in the paranormal. This force or energy would need to discharge after the event which would account for the disarray of the bedding in her room, and the marks on her arm were probably caused by a power source leaving her body.

It is possible that an Alien Intelligence far advanced than planet Earth can scientifically recreate a Paranormal event, but searching for what? It appears obvious that any alien in humanoid form will be like earthlings, limited by the capabilities of their body, the only answer to which is to transfer into a Cyborg form - indestructible, self-repairing robotic eternal life. The problem is that human DNA would continue to fade away, and need to be refreshed. Furthermore, aliens may be aware that the Powers of the Universe – God, is the only link to the origin of everything, and without that link there is no protection whatsoever from undesirable powers of the Paranormal.

Tracey Fletcher's case is important, because it points towards a scientific maize. What are the dangers that emerge from Alien Abductions in the physical or the paranormal either in the present or in future time; what are advanced aliens searching for, or planning to take from planet Earth. Are alien forces from our galaxy, solar system, a break-through from another dimension, such as the Paranormal or future time.

It is possible that Aliens are not revealing either themselves or their purpose because they see a planet full of primitive humanoids; some societies where the men are allowed, without punishment, to murder either their wives or daughters. Other so called advanced societies where murderers and rapists are not allowed to be deported to their country of origin because of a rule that allows them a family life. Other large parts of the planet Earth are constantly in the chaos of war brought about by Dictatorship of mad men still trapped in the dark ages, and will never learn that the only intelligent way of gaining the ascendance is through economic achievements, and not war. Aliens are certainly not here for what they can learn from earthlings, on a planet Earth, a planet that has only a future in the apocalyptic.

Alien phenomenon must be taken seriously because its potential danger to planet Earth is not understood. History is full of evidence that it is the most obscure threats that spring the biggest surprises, because most world leaders do not have the time to analyse every potential threat in absolute detail, but make decisions on incomplete analysis that leads to many world leaders over history making the wrong or a disastrous decision/s. Illustrated clearly in modern times by the threat to human kind, animals and insects from the dangers of Global Warming that has fetched the Sixth Mass Extinction which is now well under way, and cannot be stopped, only modified, part of the apocalyptic future for humanoids and animals; creatures in this age for planet Earth.

THE SECRETS OF THE UNIVERSE
SUN LIN

I know that you like me Ronald, have seen the ultimate, the secrets of the Universe. That the real God is the Powers of the Universe, the Intelligence of the Universe, the Spirit of Transmission across the whole Universe. The ultimate Power, and Consciousness of the Universe. Not a man sitting on the throne in a place called Heaven, that Jesus said is invisible. Existing only in the minds of early religiose; a myth that has served mankind for two thousand years has been pushed aside by Scientific discoveries in Astrophysics and Astronomy. So too has the idea that God in Heaven, somewhere in the skies, can Reincarnate to be born on Earth, and Reincarnate again on death, back into Heaven, somewhere in the sky, is a myth, but really does happen in the Paranormal. A beautiful touching story now replaced in the modern world by the truth of the Paranormal, Instantaneous across the Universe, and is a shadow attached to every individual for life; recording everything throughout life and determines the route after Death to

Reincarnation, or time spent with the Unredeemed Dead. Also pushes aside the notion that one man can forgive another man's sins, without the sinner themselves going through true personal repentance, is a nonsense of great proportion.

It would be a tragedy to lose our Churches, and I urge everyone to support their local church, of whatever denomination, and Mosque, at least during annual celebration, or other important religious events, by at least donating some money, if their time is of the essence. I fear, however, with the failure of Churches to modernise their doctrine, will eventually lead to them become places for Marriages, Burials, and Christenings only, and hopefully a wide range of other useful services to help their local community such as Food Banks, quality Citizens Advice, staffed by devout, unpaid trained volunteers who love God. My other strong opinion is that sectarian style church should be banned from preaching to the vulnerable on doorsteps.

SUN LIN GIVES ADVICE TO RUSSIA

I suggest that the simplest solution for reviving the Russian economy and fetching it closer to Europe after the collapse of oil and gas prices and the ravages of Covid 19, is to give Russian Citizens living in state owned homes the Freehold ownership of their home to sell, let, or lease their property in whichever area they live, free of any cost, except Stamp Duty. Such a move should set the Russian Economy alight. The same privilege should be extended to the Farming Industry, to attract foreign capital, and ownership, to that section of Russian economy. State planning rules should also be varied to enable residents to extend their homes.

I know Ronald, that you worked in the team that achieved Independence for Ukraine, and working with the CIA and the Ukrainian KGB. You learned quickly that the mind-set of Russian nationals, are very different to other parts of Europe.

Yes Sun Lin, I also lived in Hong Kong where I met with the Chinese Secret Police, before the change-over in Hong Kong. There I learnt that the mind-set of Chinese nationals is different to nationals in every other part of the world. I lived in Italy, a different world altogether.

Nothing will ever stop 'anti-other nationals' rhetoric, but the ultimate answer is to become a trading partner with supposed enemies. Choose that course and world economies will expand and enemies may eventually **become** friends, to the benefit of all; overcome differences and talk to each other.

THE SKULL OF DOOM

On returning from my visit to Sun Lin, I saw the Skull of Doom standing, feet planted firmly on the ground, with a face looking increasingly scary than when I saw him last. A DEADLY WARNING! Ronald, you are my favourite Prophet in all the world. You have faithfully recorded my words of warning in your books over the past ten years. All of my predictions to the letter have been one hundred percent correct. I have warned the people on the planet that the Sixth Mass Extinction, brought about by human kind is well under way, and gathering pace; confirmed when the permafrost in Siberia melts, placing that whole country at risk. However, the world will not be completely destroyed by flood Ronald, but Pandemics will change Earth.

The peoples of the earth have lost their way Ronald, and I will smite the peoples of planet Earth with my Pandemics, but listen still Ronald, a new warning; On top of my plagues, I will smite World Economies, fetching darkness and gross darkness upon the peoples of my Earth. The phenomenal economic rise since the Industrial Revolution in the eighteenth century has reached its peak, and will turn over like a head-and-shoulders on the side of a mountain over these next years, when the world will become over borrowed, and many world economies will become a shadow of their former selves. Pandemics will result in smaller populations through falling birth rates, fewer jobs, fewer business, everything is going to change. Planet Earth is out of balance and this will bring bad events upon the peoples of the Earth.

My Reverberating and Liquifying **Earthquakes** shall smite the Earth, and I repeat; DARKNESS SHALL COVER THE PEOPLES OF THE EARTH. I will smite anyone who tries to cause any harm to you in anyway, Ronald, including your neighbours upon the Earth. Don't cry for those that try to harm you Ronald, for I have already sealed the cancers and diseases within their bodies for which there will be no cure or escape. None of their prayers shall be answered.

I have much work to carry through Ronald. I have been destroying those Satans on Earth who claim to speak in the name of God but disobey Gods very Commandment: "THOU SHALL NOT KILL". I have been destroying their Villages and Towns, by War and by Earthquakes, and scattered their peoples across the planet. They will have no home. I will not relent until they stop killing the innocents in MY NAME.

Before I go Ronald, I have to tell you. The next big leap in human evolution has arrived. Human-kind has become super humankind, as the human brain of individuals become connected through mobile phones to the most powerful Computer Technology ever.

This jump in human evolution is imperative, because over population is destroying the planet. The Sixth Mass Extinction cannot be stopped, neither can the Pandemics striking everywhere across the planet, time after time. Super technology and super human individuals will help human kind survive the ravages until the next Ice Age, after which the planet will be renewed once more. The sex mating instinct of all creatures ensures that over population cannot be stopped and so there is no hope of fetching Global Warming under human control. Do not believe those who tell you otherwise Ronald. The horizon of Earth is Chaos, because Pandemics change thinking causes break down in Law and Order everywhere, into most nations across the planet. There will be looting, fires, everywhere, because politicians will take too long to recruit and train: Paramilitary Law Enforcement Officers that will be necessary to seize control of law and order. Tell your readers Ronald, to follow the advice in your books since 2012. Stock up on food and drink, sufficient to last from one moon to the next, and allow no one to take it from you.

THE EVOLUTION OF THE
BODY OF HUMAN KIND HAS STALLED
PANDEMICS CHANGE THE WAY PEOPLE THINK

Another message Ronald, the evolution of human kind is log scale, and has now come up against the end - stop. Advanced technology will take over where human evolution has slowed, to enable human kind to continue, but Pandemics change everything! Highly populated countries such as India, Brazil, Pakistan will be devastated by the deaths through all ages fetched by the Corona Virus.

PORTENTS AND PARANORMAL
Next 40 years

December 2012 and 2020 marked important stages in world history for those who regard PORTENTS as of ominous significance.

Paranormal Convergence

1. December 2012 - The close of the Mayan long count calendar cycle.
2. December 2020 -The Great conjunction between Jupiter and Saturn. A portent for egregious changes across the world.
3. The coming of the opening of the Sixth Seal of Revelations.

Economic and financial problems across the planet will fetch higher food prices and shortages, accompanied with higher unemployment. World economies will become over borrowed, causing a risk to stability from the trio: Those who have nothing. Those who have very little. Those who have it all.

The Covid Pandemic will fetch

change in peoples' behaviour. People will become increasingly concerned about their survival, particularly young people who will be stressed by finding employment, and will rail against the bitter fruit of the truth of the true reality for their future, compared to the promises made by politicians and governments. Harsh policing will fetch social unrest, breakdowns in Law and Order in even the most developed countries; violent riots, setting fires, looting high streets, violent demonstrations.

Countries that have reduced policing to save money, will be in serious danger. The economic costs of the criminal damage will be far greater than money saved. Standard Policing will need to change. Former military personnel including SAS, Paratroopers, and Commandoes will need to be recruited to form a Paramilitary Police Units, equipped with helicopters to rush them to areas where organised rioting is taking place. Men who are not afraid to take on Gypsy sites, and armed rioters, because they are trained to actually enjoy the challenge.

Laws will need to change. In the UK, for example, criminals and drunks have taken to fighting policeman and actually injuring Police, knowing that there is little more risk for their behaviour than a 'fine' and perhaps 'community service,' truly letting down our brave policemen and police women. Not the fault of UK's brilliant Home Secretary, Priti Patel, (at the time of writing) but Magistrates Courts that do not realise protecting Police is a PRIORITY. Any criminals who fight or attacks police with physical blows or strangulations MUST KNOW THAT THEY FACE AN AUTOMATIC CUSTODIAL SENTENCE, WHETHER IMMEDIATE OR SUSPENDED, whether they were drunk or sober, or taking drugs. Everyone who gives false information to Police, wasting a substantial amount of police time should automatically face a substantial Fine.

CRIME IN THE UK REDUCED AT A STROKE. IN THEORY AT LEAST

If every County Council in the UK funded their Police Force to buy unmarked vans equipped with ANPR cameras, manned by part time or retired Police Men and Women, in plain clothes to visit every street, and cul-de-sac, in every town and village, these units would uncover vehicles with no Registered Keeper used in crime, and order the immediately removal. Uncover vehicles with no Insurance or Road Tax. Immediately Clamp those vehicles; deliver a Statutory Notice to the Keepers' address, giving 72 hours to provide to their nearest Police Station, proof of Insurance, or the vehicle would be seized. Proof of Road Tax for the offending vehicle or the vehicle would also be seized. WHEN WILL SOMEONE TELL POLICE FORCES ACROSS THE WORLD – NOT TO SHOOT TO KILL – GAIN CONTROL BY 'DISABLE. As a 'Marksman' I know it's possible.

PROBABLE SUCCESSFUL END RESULT

Fewer high speed chases involving Police vehicles. Fewer cars without a Registered Keeper. Fewer Uninsured vehicles on the roads. Recovery of Road Tax for the DVLA. A superior Panorama for County Police Forces by revealing the true extent of crime in their County, proving that policing in the UK may be underfunded.

Something else that strikes me as odd about Policing, after watching Police Programmes on television. Some police patrol vehicles will have two constables. One with, say, seventeen years impeccable service, and his colleague say three years-service. Surely, after say, seventeen-years-service, that officer should be a SENIOR CONSTABLE WITH ONE STRIPE, AND AFTER SAY, TWENTY-FIVE YEARS SERVICE, made A DEPUTY SERGEANT WITH TWO STRIPES. In any organisation there must be tangible rewards for long service, including pay scale/status. Why are not the very best Chief Constables elevated to The House of Lords? I would like to express thanks on behalf of the people of Essex for the Excellent job by the Police during Lockdown.

THE SIXTH SEAL

The opening of the sixth seal will trigger a new phenomenon - 'reverberating earthquakes' brought on by ice melt and planet Earth spinning faster. 'Darkness shall cover the Earth'

OF IMMEDIATE AND FUTURE CONCERN

I have warned in my books for the past eight years that Global Warming will fetch eccentric winter weather. Countries that have not experienced freezing temperatures will be hit by ten days to two - week periods of minus 21-22 degrees Celsius. Countries that rely on wind power for their electricity - Windmills will freeze. There will be no electricity for millions reliant on Wind Power. There will be heatwaves and droughts. Please remember that whilst alternative ways of producing electricity are becoming essential – the Sun does not always shine, and the Wind does not always blow.

WARS AND RUMOURS OF WARS

There is no doubt that there still exists in the world today the danger of Nuclear War.

The most potent military power in the world today is the USA. America has the most advanced military aircraft, submarines, aircraft carriers, intercontinental ballistic missiles that go into space and drop down anywhere in the world before anyone is fully aware it is coming.

China is another important military power, but does not have the advanced weapons the USA can field. China is different in that at full stretch; China could field 2,000,000 soldiers. With that many soldiers, each soldier an independent military unit, carrying their own weapons and food. No Country could defeat China. The best that could be achieved would be 'stalemate'. With their advanced aircraft and advanced weaponry, USA could annihilate any country in the world except China, who has the advantage of sheer force of numbers. In my Army days I decoded messages from Korea stating that as soon as enemy soldiers were killed or wounded, they were replaced four-fold overnight by Chinese in North Korean uniforms.

WITH THE NEW FOUND FRIENDSHIP OF CHINA IRAN WILL BECOME A NEW NORTH KOREA IN THE MIDDLE EAST

AND BECOME A REAL DANGER

TO WORLD PEACE

IRAN would like to dominate the Middle East, destroy Israel, and threaten their enemies with Nuclear Weapons, but if Iran fired a Nuclear weapon at Israel, the USA would react immediately, and Iran would be a country of smoke and ashes. Never-the-less, look at the new confidence by Iran, telling everyone to get lost, and pushing on to build a Nuclear Weapon. What has changed? The Chinese are too intelligent to be interested in war, its priority is to   dominate the world with its economic might. China has always wanted to get a foothold in the Middle East Oil to fuel its expansion, and China is now taking oil from Iran. China has all the technology to fuel Iran's ambitions, and help other Middle East countries economically. Iran will get its Nuclear weapon, and become the new 'North Korea' in the Middle East. Another weapon with which China can threaten the world by Proxy

NORTH KOREA; China has used North Korea to threaten the USA for years. If North Korea, in a moment of insanity, launched a nuclear weapon at the USA, retaliations would be immediate, and North Korea would be a desert of smoke and ashes. China is a world economic power, but is not going to give everything away to start a nuclear war with USA. Nor would the USA want to start a nuclear war with China, because the end result would be stalemate.

The rivalry between USA and China to become the world's dominant economic power will fetch tensions continuously, because China will use its might to take control of coastal waters belonging to small Island Nations because it can, particularly around Taiwan in order to continue to threaten Taiwan.

World military leaders continue to speculate about the nuclear threat from RUSSIA, but Russia has neither the money or the weaponry to take on the USA or NATO. As to recent events, I was involved with the Team that brought about Independence of UKRAINE (read my book- Joseph escapes to Glastonbury on: Amazon Kindle) working with the KGB and CIA. I always knew that Russia would seize back control of the Black Sea Ports that housed Russia's Navy. Using the guise of Russia Separatists. That is exactly what Russia achieved. The Russians did, however, own that area prior to the Second World War. Ukraine was always known as Russia's 'Bread Basket' with its two climates, and many crops. However, I am confident that other than defending itself from attack, Russia would never use its nuclear arsenal, but continue to use stealth, and creeping tactics to re-establish influence in its former territories, and creep further into its former 'bread basket' Ukraine, continuously threatening by leaving large number of troops and weapons on the Borders. President Putin has to be seen as a strong independent leader, taking on the mantle of his predecessors but, he is very intelligent, although still a threat, because he must to be seen by his peoples to be strong and fearless leader after Stalin. President Putin knows that he can steal the world stage by looking like "Russia is going to invade". Unless and until some genius can persuade President Putin, now in Office until 2036, that Russia's most prosperous future lies in becoming a trading partner with Europe, and Scandinavia, in preference to fighting or frightening them. Other countries must fetch President Putin into the fold, and not become enemies. Russia is a potential goldmine for future exports from Europe and the UK.

PANDEMICS

I warned about the coming of Pandemics in my books. At the time of writing, UK Prime Minister Boris Johnson, achieved wonders by ensuring that the UK had more Vaccine doses ordered than achieved by any other world leader, and drove an amazing Vaccination Program, literally treating 32,000,000; including the most vulnerable, in weeks, and the whole population of the UK in a few months. Boris Johnson truly leads the world; a first - class political leader praised across the world. Albeit that the UK was 'dogged' at the start of the Pandemic by housing the most obese population in Europe. The highest number with Type two Diabetes, plus a large population of ethnic groups vulnerable to Covid. The EU on the other hand, fogged by bureaucracy, remain many months behind the UK and Russia in Vaccinating its peoples, scaring citizens away from being Vaccinated because some EU leaders are telling everyone that the Vaccine could be dangerous. At the time of writing, some EU Countries have been swamped with cases of Corona Virus, and forced into Lockdowns, and no overseas travel. Serious weaknesses in the EU have been exposed during Covid. Quite incapable on reaching consensus on which Vaccine to use. Very slow in Vaccinating Citizens.

Flooding Snow and Ice for UK and Europe
Prolonged Drought for America

Flooding for Australia

I warned in my books that hurricanes attacking the USA's East Coast would double in number; the tail end of those hurricanes will cross the Atlantic hitting Ireland, the West Coast of England, running up to Scotland. Again, I warned about increased rainfall in the UK, one month's rainfall falling in one to two days; will link farmland in the West of the UK into lakes.

As predicted in our previous books, UK Winter weather will be colder due to ice melt in the Arctic slowing the Atlantic Conveyor, and resulting in Colder Winters and Snow in Spring Europe-wide, effecting crops and food output in Europe. Be warned that one month's snow could fall in two days.

In 2012 I warned that the start of the 'Mayan Long Count Calendar' would cause the drought area for America to moved 1750 miles, and will now hit California for the next 740 years. California could disappear as a habitable zone. Time to move.

Australia is not out of the woods after devastation by fires. This will now be followed by floods.

TIME TO MOVE IN THE UK AWAY
FROM THE WEST

If you are fed up with the rainfall and flooding, which will not go away, now is the time to move to the Rayner Triangle - less rainfall, more sunshine, greater prospects for jobs, and a bright future for entrepreneurs.

Take a line from Dorset in the West across to below Norfolk in the South. A line dropping to Dover and returning to Dorset. Move into this triangle, preferably not more than 40/60 miles from London, and your future will be brighter, happier; sporting a golden tan. No more misery existing in a wet and windy zone. One must weigh this against the plans by the Conservative Party to move many jobs into the Regions, which is taking place at the time of writing.

THE END OF DAYS

Planet Earth, and its Solar system, continuously circling the Universe over extended periods of thousands of years. Earth passing through showers of meteoroids bombarding planet Earth, causing rapid climate change that destroys advanced civilisations in as little as two hundred years. Climate change similar to today's Sixth Mass Extinction. Drought, heatwaves, loss of crops, starvation, and sea level rise. The disappearance of the Maya is a classic example.

My Scrying indicates that planet Earth could be travelling through a dangerous region of space that could mark 'the end of days', for the populations still alive on planet Earth until that time.

1. **PREDICTING A BOOM FOR MANY BUT UNCERTAINTY FOR SECTORS SCARED BY LOCKDOWNS.**

2. **A BREAKDOWN IN LAW AND ORDER BY YOUNG PEOPLE ACROSS THE UK**

3. **NEWSPAPERS SHOULD REVIEW THE UK STOCK MARKETS AGAINST WIDE SCALE OVER BORROWING**

4. **REVIEW THE TRUE PICTURE FOR PROPERTY COMPANIES WITH EMPTY SHOPS IN TOWN CENTRES/MOTHBALLED IN LONDON**

5. **A POTENTIAL FALL IN ATTRACTIVENESS OF COMPANIES USING WIDESPREAD 'HOME WORKING'.**

6. **COMPANIES SCARED BY LOCKDOWNS' WILL TAKE THREE TO FIVE YEARS TO RECOVER. WAREHOUSING WILL BOOM**

7. **THE SIXTH MASS EXTINCTION WILL CONTINUE UNABATED ACROSS THE WORLD WITH FIRES, FLOODING, DROUGHTS, FAMINE ETC, PLUS ECCENTRIC WEATHER.**

MUCH OF WHAT WE KNEW IN THE PAST WILL CHANGE FOREVER

Normal routines followed by many shops and businesses will change forever, as the result of the coming of the Corona virus, plus the surprising number of companies in the UK giving workers the choice of working from home or splitting Home or working in Company Offices. Companies that use their Head Offices just for their administrative and accounting core will reduce footfall in Town Centres by twenty percent. When one includes the negative effects wrought by the explosion in on-line shopping, around 200,000 jobs will be lost to the retail industries. On-line shopping will grow to a high of sixty seven percent, damaging further the employment prospects in retail. One important under estimate of the consequence resulting from the on-line shopping, is a necessary re-evaluation of Town centre properties, and other retail office space in the regions. This will change the outlook for some, but warehousing will boom.

I know from personal experience as a Managing Dealer in the City of London, that without discipline some staff lose the plot completely, and become lazy. This will apply particularly to people working from home, whereas in an office environment there is spontaneity, team building, innovation about ways to increase company growth and profits. Home working will lead to loss of growth and profits, resulting in companies becoming seriously overborrowed Zombie companies.

SCRYING THE FUTURE OF WORK FROM HOME

THERE IS A DARK AND POTENTIALLY SINISTER SHADOW FROM FUTURE TIME OVERHANGING THE WORK FROM HOME CULTURE. The Shadow. Some companies may be encouraging their work-from-home culture to eventually force those working from home to switch to SELF EMPLOYMENT, enabling companies to reap the massive savings – ridding themselves of the huge cost of National Insurance Payments, Pension Contributions, Sickness Benefits, Holiday Pay, and providing expensive office space.

THE FUTURE OUTLOOK FOR FULL AND PART TIME EMPLOYMENT IS GRIM, PROBABLY THE WORST FOR MANY YEARS BUT NO FAULT OF GOVERNMENT POLICIES.

Quite apart from the damage done to the Hospitality Industries, and the massive damage caused by on-line shopping with a potential total loss of 222,000 retail jobs, the annual waves of graduates leaving universities, plus other students exiting full-time education, will swamp what few jobs will be available for 16/25 year age groups. Some may never work.

If Governments want to avoid a breakdown in law and order across the UK, amongst groups of young people, who are our children, grandchildren, and great grandchildren; they matter very much. Governments must give them hope of a future if we are not to lose them to drug taking and crime and disorder. Open SCHOOLS of TRAINING for every youngster without entry qualification, and pay our young children ten pounds a day for attending classes. This is an important issue, these are our children, and our future!

COVID AND LOCKDOWNS COULD FETCH SOME REORIENTATION IN THE PROPERTY SECTOR

Between Twenty-five to fifty percent of Rents could be lost as a result of the massive switch to online shopping. Many rents will be reduced by thirty per cent. Some property companies with empty shops in Town Centres and elsewhere may be advised to reorientate themselves as; Property and Property Development Companies. Redevelop empty shops to FLATS for lease, rent or sale. Such a change could give a very bright future for some companies, and give permanent footfall in Town Centres/Warehouses.

THE TREE OF LIFE
THE SECRET GARDEN

The Gates Opened

At last, the Secret Garden

The Garden of Gethsemane

I open my Third Eye

And a Heavenly Glow surrounded me

The Olive Tree

The Tree of Life

Stood over me

Below the trees Saffron Monks slept peacefully

To greet the day' I made Sweet Tea

With the healing leaves of my tree

I filled each wooden bowl with olives

The fruit of the tree

The little garden was silent

Quietly the large snowflakes began to fall,

Covering the Monks and the ground they walked on

The trees glistening in the sunlight

Once again, the silence.

THE MAGIC BEGINS

The Secret of the Olive Groves

A golden glow covered the men as they entered

the snow-covered garden

Whispering as they made their way to the grotto

Where it is written

They rested and slept

Dedicated to the keepers of Gethsemane.

Poetry lifts the every day into the extroardinary

FEAR NOT TOMORROW GOD IS ALREADY THERE

CHANGE WHO YOU ARE IN SEVEN DAYS -
Ultimate success achieved from
Meditation and Mindfulness

Meditation and Mindfulness gradually shrinks the person inside us we secretly not want to be, by expanding the person inside us we should be, and want to become, by fully connecting our Conscious Mind to our Subconscious Mind developing expanded consciousness, and awareness, with emotional balance.

Overtime there emerges both within us, and outwardly, a more confident New Self, from the acquisition of Divine Knowledge: not afraid of what the future may bring because we have become confident that everything will be overcome, and that victory can be snatched from defeat, with the certain knowledge that even Death can be overcome through reincarnation.

No longer will our fully understanding newly born self, permit others to worry us, or trouble us, or influence our new life that pursues meaningful activities, by doing everything in the right way because it fetches best results, and demonstrates to others around us that there is an Exit from their own evolutionary cul-de-sac in which they have been trapped, releasing into the world the goodness and love in all sane people.

DEMAND A NOBEL PRIZE FOR UK
PRIME MINISTER BORIS JOHNSON

The Covid Pandemic is probably the biggest tragedy most people will witness in their lifetime, particularly the extent of the effect in India. The UK was saved from the extent of the terrible tragedy on the scale of India, for example, by the actions of one man; Prime Minister Boris Johnson, who ordered millions of doses of Vaccine ahead of the rest of the world. Took action to obtain sufficient Ventilators, saving thousands of lives every month in the UK. Going on to Vaccinate all vulnerable citizens in the UK in weeks, and vaccinating the whole population in a few months. Considerably faster than the EU, and any other country in the world. The first to send Aid to our Indian Friends. What a magnificent achievement for the whole population of the UK, and India. The man is a Saint, and should be rewarded by nothing less than a NOBEL PRIZE. I urge all fair minded readers to write to their favourite newspaper, and support this quest.

ALIEN MONK SUN LIN – PREDICTS THAT SCOTTISH INDEPENDENCE IS A DISASTER OUT THERE IN FUTURE TIME WAITING TO HAPPEN TO THE PEOPLES OF SCOTLAND. IS ALSO EXTREMELY DANGEROUS TO THE SECURITY OF THE UK AND NATO.

During my last visit to Alien Monk Sun Lin, in Tibet, I asked him for his Predictions for Scotland following a Referendum for Scottish Independence from the United Kingdom. Sun Lin's Predictions are so stark and troublesome for both the people of Scotland and the Security for the UK and NATO I have left these pages for the end of this book.

"Ronald, I have been scrying into future Time for Scotland using my Crystal skull. The picture is very serious for the people of Scotland and the Security of the UK and NATO. The UK saying NO to Scotland will be ignored by Scottish Politicians, and they will go ahead to Vote for Independence.

SCOTTISH ECONOMY WILL COLLAPSE

Scotland, Ronald, has neither the GDP or Finances to support an Independent Scotland. Scotland will demand a large part of the Bank of England's Reserves that they have not earned or to which they have no entitlement what so ever to support Independence.
A vibrant and booming Scottish economy will collapse, as Banks and Financial Institutions, Oil and Gas Companies leave Scotland, taking their jobs with them to the UK. Banks and others because Scotland does not have the money to support them in the event of another world Banking Crisis, or Quantitative Easing.

UK COMPANIES WILL BE NATIONALISED TO KEEP MONEY AND JOBS IN SCOTLAND

Companies and organisations Fear they will be Nationalised by the new Scottish Government to keep their money and jobs in Scotland.

IN A DESPERATE SITUATION SCOTLAND COULD GRAB THE UK'S NUCLEAR BASES AND CHARGE THE UK BILLIONS TO KEEP THEM IN PLACE TO RAISE MONEY

I have always held the view that the UK's Army, Navy, and Airforce are always vital, not only to defend the UK but to save the UK from itself if any MPs or groups tried to gain control of the UK. It is possible Ronald, that trapped in a desperate situation Ronald, an Independent Scottish Government would try to persuade the Scottish Regiments to switch loyalties to them, in order to gain control where they felt it was needed.

RUSSIA AND CHINA WOULD OFFER TO LEND MONEY AND RESOURCES TO SCOTLAND ENDANGERING UK SECURITY AND NATO

The other great danger Ronald to the security of the UK and NATO, is a desperate Scotland looking at offers of money from Russia and China, to enable Russia and China to gain a foothold on UK soil.

AN INDEPENDENT SCOTLAND COULD SEIZE SHIPS UNDER CONSTRUCTION TO FORM ITS OWN INDEPENDENT NAVY

The most important consideration in such a debacle is that the UK stays together for both strength and security, with a booming economy, and prosperous economic future, and able to defend itself in an increasingly unsecure world, and to support its brothers and sister across the world, such as India in times of need.

Scottish people should look to the facts. Prime Minister Boris Johnson saved thousands of lives in Scotland, and the rest of the UK by buying sufficient Vaccine to Immunise everyone in the England, Wales, Scotland, and Northern Ireland, faster than any country in the world. Bought up Ventilators. Helped families survive with Furlough Payments and other schemes. An Independent Scotland would never have the money to achieve the brilliant success achieved by Boris Johnson and his Team. The UK is a family Ronald, and families that break up inevitably end in disaster, usually for the party that splits.

INDEX

PRAYERS FOR EVERYONE IN THE WORLD OF ANY FAITH OR BELIEF

May the Face of your GOD to your own personal Belief or Religion

BLESS ME……………Your Name THIS DAY

Repeat out loud or mentally in any place or time

PLEASE KEEP ME FREE FROM HARM, INJURY, OR ILLNESS. GUIDE ME, AND HELP ME, AND LEAD ME IN EVERYTHING I DO WRITE OR SAY, PLEASE FETCH ANSWERS TO MY PRAYERS, HOPES AND WISHES FOR MYSELF AND MY FAMILY, AND BRING ME GOOD FORTUNE IN THE DAYS, WEEKS AND MONTHS AHEAD.

This really does work. Repeat as frequently as is convenient. Hold Hands